The Artistic Vision

The Artistic Vision

*Cultivating a Sacramental Imagination
for Creative Practice*

ALEX SOSLER
GARY BALL

CASCADE *Books* · Eugene, Oregon

THE ARTISTIC VISION
Cultivating a Sacramental Imagination for Creative Practice

Cascade Books
An Imprint of Wipf and Stock Publishers
199 W. 8th Ave., Suite 3
Eugene, OR 97401

www.wipfandstock.com

PAPERBACK ISBN: 978-1-6667-6013-2
HARDCOVER ISBN: 978-1-6667-6014-9
EBOOK ISBN: 978-1-6667-6015-6

Cataloguing-in-Publication data:

Names: Sosler, Alex, author. | Ball, Gary, author.

Title: The artistic vision : cultivating a sacramental imagination for creative practice / Alex Sosler and Gary Ball.

Description: Eugene, OR: Cascade Books, 2024 | Includes bibliographical references.

Identifiers: ISBN 978-1-6667-6013-2 (paperback) | ISBN 978-1-6667-6014-9 (hardcover) | ISBN 978-1-6667-6015-6 (ebook)

Subjects: LCSH: Christianity and the arts. | Sacraments—History of doctrines. | Spiritual life.

Classification: BR115.A8 A775 2024 (print) | BR115.A8 (ebook)

From Gary:
To my wife Susannah,
a patient and steady presence, who is mother
to four of God's most beautiful masterpieces

From Alex:
To Lauren,
the beauty that leads me to God

Everything around us is sacramental, in the sense that everything God has created both points to him and makes him present.

—Hans Boersma, *Scripture as Real Presence*

I asked what would be the thoughts of a man who, when examining a flower, or herb, or a pebble, or a ray of light, which he treats as something so beneath him the scale of existence, suddenly discovered that he was in the presence of some powerful being who was hidden behind the visible things he was inspecting.

—John Henry Newman, *Apologia 77*

The chance sight of a flower illumined by the sun's rays or of the starry heavens, the moon and the stars which God has ordained, impress the feeling of God upon the soul more than any artificial reasoning from final causes. Like the centurion by the Cross we are awed into belief.

—Edward Pusey, *Parochial Sermons*

There is a book, who runs may read,
 Which heavenly truth imparts,
And all the lore its scholars need,
 Pure eyes and Christian hearts.

The works of God above, below,
 Within us and around,
Are pages in that book, to show
 How God Himself is found . . .

. . . Thou, who hast given me eyes to see
 And love this sight so fair,
Give me a heart to find out Thee,
 And read Thee everywhere.
—John Keble, "Septuagesima Sunday"

My task which I am trying to achieve is, by the power of the written word, to make you hear, to make you feel—it is before all, to make you *see*. That—and no more, and it is everything.

—Flannery O'Connor, *Mystery and Manners*

Table of Contents

Illustrations

Introduction

I appeal especially to you, Christian artists: I wish to remind each of you that, beyond functional considerations, the close alliance that has always existed between the Gospel and art means that you are invited to use your creative intuition to enter into the heart of the mystery of the Incarnate God and at the same time into the mystery of man.

Letter of His Holiness Pope John Paul II to Artists, §14

Because children have abounding vitality, because they are in spirit fierce and free, therefore they want things repeated and unchanged. They always say, "Do it again"; and the grown-up does it again until he is nearly dead. For grown-up people are not strong enough to exult in monotony. But perhaps God is strong enough to exult in monotony. It is possible that God says every morning, "Do it again" to the sun; and every evening, "Do it again" to the moon. It may not be automatic necessity that makes all daisies alike; it may be that God makes every daisy separately but has never got tired of making them. It may be that He has the eternal appetite of infancy; for we have sinned and grown old, and our Father is younger than we.

–G. K. Chesterton, *Orthodoxy*

THIS IS WATER

There's nothing more important than how you see the world.

In a graduation address to Kenyon College, the novelist David Foster Wallace opened with an illustration about fish and water. You may have heard it before. There are two younger fish swimming along, when an older fish passes by and says, "Hey boys. How's the water?" The younger fish swim along when one of them looks at the other and asks, "What the hell is water?"[1]

How you see the world may be as confusing and strange a question as "How's the water?" is to fish. The way we see the world, Wallace goes on to argue, is our default setting. There's nothing wrong with a default setting. We all have one. Fish don't question the water because that's the context in which they live. It's the air they breathe, the proverbial water they swim in. It's natural. The sinister thing about a default setting is how unquestioned and how self-centered our default setting often is.

The question of how you see the world is an aesthetic question. It deals with the way things appear to us and what we make of them. Being an aesthetic question, then, it is also a pertinent question for artists. How you see the world has been shaped and formed even if you have never considered how you see the world, the water you swim in. Perhaps you were raised in the church, and the church cultivated a sense of the fallenness of the world. What you see in the world is danger. The world is something to be feared and guarded against. Or maybe art school has reshaped the way you see the world. The world is not a danger but a playground. Not only objects but feelings ought to be shown and displayed without question.

Parents, institutions, churches, schools, friends: these all shape the way we see the world—the water we swim in—our default setting.

So, this is a book about the way we look at the world. It's a book about water.

The Courage to See

Towards the end of Marilynne Robinson's novel *Gilead,* Reverend Ames, the fictional pastor from Gilead, Iowa, wrote to his young son, "But the Lord is more constant and far more extravagant than it seems to imply. Wherever you turn your eyes the world can shine like transfiguration. You don't have to bring a thing to it except a willingness to see. Only who could have the courage to see?"[2] Here, the aged reverend beckons Jesus' transfiguration in the company of Peter, James, and John. He says the whole world—from the stars and the moon to the atom and molecule—shines like transfiguration. We only must be willing to see it.

1. Wallace, "This Is Water."
2. Robinson, *Gilead,* 243.

Who could have the courage to see? That's a great question. At the heart of the Christian consciousness is the hope to see God—that's the Christian's ultimate destiny. Theologians call it the beatific vision. In Christ, we all end up gazing at the beauty of the Lord. In the meantime, we get glimpses. With Gerard Manley Hopkins, we can see the world "charged with the grandeur of God"—because it is. The world shines like transfiguration. But if we're honest, the world often doesn't appear that way. Perhaps the fall has taken too deep of a hold. Perhaps we're too distracted or preoccupied to see. Maybe, we don't have the necessary courage.

The courage to see God is an interesting idea. It suggests that it is our own doubt or weakness that hinders us from seeing God in created things. "Surely, God can't be found here," we may subconsciously think. Maybe we've become smitten with American Christianity, which Michael Horton describes as a story of perpetual upheavals in churches and individual lives. Starting with the extraordinary conversion experience, our lives are motivated by a constant expectation for the Next Big Thing. We're growing bored with the ordinary means of God's grace, attending church week in and week out. Doctrines which are disciplines that have shaped faithful Christian witness in the past are often marginalized or substituted with newer fashions or methods. The new and improved may dazzle us for a moment, but soon they have become "so last year."[3] Often, we are trained to see God in the new and novel rather than the ancient or ordinary.

Where are you looking to see God? Where do you find him? Can anything of God's creation be absent from the Creator's mark?

SEGMENTING OURSELVES

We write concerned about the waters many artists swim in—not necessarily fearful of the boogeyman of culture "out there." There are unhealthy waters of reductionism and fragmentation. So often, there is an intentional disconnect between an artist's faith and their art—and the challenge both comes from culture and Christian culture.

An artist's vocation is a challenging concept. Vocation, stemming from the Latin *vocare*, has to do with a calling and a caller. In the words of Frederick Buechner, it has something to do with the calling of our deep gladness and the calling of the world's great need. Where those two things align, you have a vocation. There's been a renewed interest in the intersection of

3. Horton, *Ordinary*, 16.

faith and work. How does one's faith impact one's work? Are they separate? Is "secular" work a sort of distraction from "religious" work? How should they be integrated, if at all? Many churches are helping their people discern and connect their faith and work. Except, it seems, for artists. Theirs is one of the few vocations with an accepted distance between faith and work. Faith ought not to impact one's work, so it seems that one's Christian faith would make one's art shallow or trivial rather than more profound and more substantial. We're sympathetic to such a notion. The novelist Dorothy Sayers suggests, "The Church's approach to an intelligent carpenter is usually confined to exhorting him not to be drunk and disorderly in his leisure hours and to come to church on Sundays. What the Church should be telling him is this: that the very first demand that his religion makes upon him is that he should make good tables."[4] Amen. There's something about being true to the craft that makes excellent art. Don't fall prey to modernism, which packages art as an idea to be understood, or to the contemporary art world that replaces art for an idea. Be excellent. Serve the craft. We don't want to say less than this. But we do want to say more.

The church where we pastor, Redeemer Anglican, is in Asheville, North Carolina. Our church was planted in this neighborhood ten years ago. We are a liturgical and sacramental parish situated in a place known for its artistic appeal. Asheville draws artists from around the country and has become a popular destination for art tourism. Historically, the culture has been influenced primarily by the arts and crafts tradition common to the Appalachian Mountains—art forms that reflect the character of this region. The cultural art of the mountains was born out of a shared experience and often combines beauty and function. However, over the last decade, a broad shift in demographics has introduced various changes in the community at large, especially in the arts. The arts have taken a materialist shift, a diminishment of embodied expression that arises from a shared experience and becomes more a reflection of the individual expression. Individualism is on the rise, especially as taste is increasingly considered to be subjective.

Our church was purposefully planted in a neighborhood most affected by these changes. It was once known as the neighborhood to avoid but has become a highly sought-after place to live and work. In many ways, our church has benefited from the changes taking place. The people who have migrated here have added to the artistic life of our church and neighborhood. Artists comprise approximately a third of our church, representing

4. Sayers, *Letters to a Diminished Church*, 77.

various ages, experiences, and genres. As we listened to artists in our community, a standard narrative emerged, namely that a separation between what they are actually doing and what they feel is central to their role as artists. For example, several expressed leading others to see God as a primary purpose of their life. However, they had trouble describing how this purpose factors into their art, with many saying that it is not reflected in their work. The separation between what many stated as their purpose and everyday practice had clearly contributed to their feeling unfulfilled. However, many could not identify an apparent reason for this sense. From the outside, it appeared to stem from confusion about how faith should be integrated with artistic practice. While many felt like faith should influence their work, it remained isolated from their practice for various reasons. Through conversations with artists, some could identify a clear relationship when art was made in or for the church. Still, a distinction was made between "church art" and art intended for a more general audience.

Our city is known for pushing cultural boundaries, and the effort to preserve the rebellious reputation of our city has bred a particular hostility toward Christianity. This implicit and explicit antagonism has made it difficult for Christians in the art world and has stifled the willingness of many artists to express themselves in a holistic way. In fact, "being found out to be a Christian" has been a common fear among artists in our congregation. For example, some expressed that being labeled as a "Christian" could jeopardize their standing in the community in a variety of ways. Common examples included losing a large portion of their audience and even limiting their ability to reserve certain venues for display. One artist was concerned that if others knew they were Christians, they would be associated with a particular political party. While some were ashamed to hide their faith, they felt it necessary to preserve their credibility in the field.

These examples demonstrate how fear can lead artists to separate any spiritual influence from their art purposefully. This isolation had become so commonplace that it was difficult for many to identify what was missing. Fear had led many to operate from a place of preservation rather than freedom, dampening their inspiration and constraining their ability to see the world through spiritual eyes. Contemporary poet John O'Donohue refers to fear as "negative wonder," stating, "fear is a force that can turn that which is real, meaningful, warm, gentle and kind in your life into devastation and desert."[5] Fear leads us to operate from a place of safety, which can limit our

5. O'Donohue, *Walking in Wonder*, 15.

anticipation of meaning beyond that which is agreeable to the onlooking world that exhibits an over-rational approach to life. This consistent mode of thinking and creating art conditions our souls and can lead us toward a crisis in our vocation.

Functioning in what many have described as a difficult environment has led many to focus on preserving their reputations and ultimately taking on the character of the culture in which they operate. This change has sometimes resulted in culture being the primary influence in forming artists. Granted, it can often feel like we have more in common with non-Christian artists, mainly because of a shared critique of Christian art. However, the result has a formative effect on our imagination. It is easy to rally people around an opposing view, which opens the door to our identity being formed around what we are not. For example, many artists attempt to distinguish themselves from other Christian art, which has created a purposeful separation. Whether we truly believe that heavenly and earthly realities can function in isolation by representing one apart from the other, our eyes are trained to see the world in such a way. In this way, Christians have been susceptible to a formalism that focuses on form as the defining mark of art, which stems from both our view of the world and shapes our view of the world. With this in mind, it seems possible to change how Christians think about art by first changing how we see the world.

So, the broader culture can affect an artist's separation of faith from art, but so too can the church and Christian culture at large. The lack of formation (or malformation) provided by the church is another obstacle to overcome for artists. Unfortunately, Christians have garnered a reputation for producing art that lacks substance. Therefore, artists often express concerns about being associated with this genre that has become known for making cheap imitations of "real" art. Because Christian art has frequently projected a view of reality that lacks integrity, it is regarded mainly as cliched, neglecting the literal, temporal reality of our existence in favor of the more palatable, disembodied, spiritual dimension. Separating themselves from this genre has had spiritual consequences related to spiritual vision. Compartmentalizing faith and practice ultimately leads us to categorize the world similarly, as either/or, rather than acknowledging the participation between spiritual and material realities. In pushing back against what they refer to as a shallow expression of art (for good reason), many artists have sought to portray all of life in an honest or authentic manner. However, by distancing themselves from the inauthentic representations that many associate with Christian art, artists have often overcorrected and, thus, unknowingly taken an over-materialist approach—focusing exclusively on earthly experience without regard to a connected spiritual meaning. Just like over-spiritualist art, materialist art has the potential to present a view of life that falls short of reality—a version of our existence that is based on an immediate felt experience or circumstances only as they appear. For example, artists might imitate the beauty of creation apart from the awareness of its source, thus representing nature not as a gift but as a pure, brute fact. Or, we might focus on brokenness or sadness without considering the layers of meaning in or beyond those moments. Sentimentality exists in both expressions, either by presenting a fantastical vision of life that suggests we "get over it," or in a way that draws people into the moment, to commiserate with the artist's grief without ever pushing beyond emotions or experiences of life to encounter hope.

Through these many conversations with artists in the church, they revealed both implicit and explicit influences that had led many artists to check their faith at the studio door. Here's our main contention: if artists isolate the most important part of their being, how can it be fulfilling? So, we seek to establish an integrative vision of life, where there is joining together rather than separating. A sacramental vision fulfills the meaning artists are seeking. The rejoining vision would naturally rejoin faith and practice; art would become a natural expression rather than contrived or inauthentic.

The beginning of this book aims to observe how the purposeful separation of our spiritual life from our earthly activity can affect how we see the world. The recovery of beauty as a central aspect of discipleship can help artists integrate faith and practice. Jesus' manner of appealing to our imagination can give us a valuable model for forming our souls and enhancing artistic composition. Truth and goodness are certainly part of divine revelation; however, Christ appeals to all our senses by describing our earthly experience as imbued with transcendent meaning. With our imaginations shaped this way, the sacramental connections between heavenly and earthly reality can be found. Artists represent the world as they see it; therefore, the discovery of its divine presence cannot be isolated from creative practices. A fully formed spiritual imagination could bring a renewed sense of fulfillment in their vocation as they see and depict a transcendent world. As artists, we see everything as a potential subject, so producing only material versions of life as we see it naturally leads us to focus on forms without acknowledging any more profound meaning. If we aren't in the habit of looking for God, it is possible, even if by accident, to come to see him as absent from creation.

Elijah and the Whisper

In 1 Kings 19, the prophet Elijah finds himself exhausted and alone. In the previous chapter, King Ahab sets up a face-off between Elijah and the prophets of Baal. Elijah offers the proposition: "If the Lord is God, follow him; but if Baal, then follow him" (18:21). Elijah is the only prophet of the Lord, and there are over 450 prophets of Baal. The task before them: call on your respective god to bring fire on the sacrifice of a bull. The prophets of Baal get to work. They prepare the bull. They set up the altar. They call on their god. They cut themselves and rave, but to no avail. Baal is silent.

After they're done, Elijah steps up. He repairs the altar of the Lord and digs a trench around it and invites people to fill the trench with water. Then he calls on the name of the Lord to bring fire. And the Lord does. He tells Ahab to leave as rain approaches. Ahab makes it back to his wife, Jezebel, to tell her all that had happened. Now, Queen Jezebel seeks Elijah's life. She makes a vow to not stop until she sees Elijah dead.

Here is where we find Elijah in 1 Kings 19. On the run and in the wilderness, he's alone and hungry and tired. In psychological terminology, he is exhibiting signs of depression. He even wishes that the Lord would take his life. We could say he has suicidal ideation. And God gives him a nap and meal: ordinary things that sustain him. The Lord directs him to leave, and he comes to a cave after forty days and forty nights on the mount of Horeb.

Here, in the cave, God asks Elijah to come out and stand on the mount. Just as with Moses' forty days on the mount, God was going to pass by Elijah. So, Elijah stands there in the open, and a great strong wind whips over the mountaintop. But, the text says, the Lord was not in the wind. Next, an earthquake shakes the very foundation that Elijah is standing on. But the Lord was not in the earthquake. Then a fire—like the burning bush that Moses saw. But the Lord was not in the fire.

Finally, the sound of a low whisper. In Hebrew, a direct translation would be "small silence."

A low whisper. A small silence. That's kind of anticlimactic, right? We look for God to show up on the mountaintop, in big, extraordinary ways—as he did with Elijah the chapter before when God sends fire to light the sacrifice, as with Moses and the burning bush. Here on the mountaintop, we expect God to show up in grandiose ways. But God decides to appear in a low whisper.

After the chaos of the drama, I imagine it was eerily quiet. When Elijah expected God to show up in the noticeable—as was God's history—Elijah heard the inconspicuous. A whisper. I've seen teachers use a similar strategy to gain the attention of students in a loud classroom. The teacher doesn't scream at the children to get their attention. Rather, he or she begins to speak with a soft voice. The students, slowly noticing, start to lean in. They are forced to quiet themselves and hush the other voices to hear what is being said. I think something like this may be happening between God and Elijah. Elijah is having to lean in and focus his attention on the voice. He must quiet the noise of his own thoughts or the distractions caused by fear and disappointment. He must attend to the moment.

These moments of ordinary revelation require attentiveness. On an ordinary day, God forms our awareness as we lean in, and he leads us to anticipate the various ways that are revealed through all creation. When we slow down, we feel the soft breeze of wind against our faces. Or we return from a full day at work, and a child greets us with a shout and a hug. Or we notice a shine of light through a window. In all these ordinary, unexpected ways, God wants to communicate to us through created things. We must bring the courage to see it.

SACRAMENTAL VISION

Seeing God in ordinary circumstances and recognizing in mundane ways is part of what we mean by a sacramental vision. As defined in the Catechism of the Book of Common Prayer (1662), a sacrament is "an outward and visible sign of an inward and spiritual grace." In the sacraments both the material and the spiritual matter. The physical bread and wine matter but not solely because of themselves. They point to and convey something beyond the mere physical elements. They signify the divine reality of Jesus' body broken and blood shed. In the same way, as artists, the physical matters. The material realities that we see and display and use are important. At the same time, we also point through and beyond them. There is something more going on than just the material.

For artists, I think there's a tendency to desire to display the phenomenal and extraordinary. We want God to show up in the miraculous. But what if we had the courage to slow down, to be attentive to our daily lives, and to have the patience to hear or "see" God in the whispers? I think that's what God wants to show us and to show us so that others may have the eyes to see God in the mundane, too.

We wrote this book for Christian artists and those who love artists. The title "Christian Artist" carries a lot of baggage. However, as Jacques Maritain says, "If you want to make a Christian work, then be Christian, and simply try to make a beautiful work. . . . Do not try to make Christian art."[6] These statements cast art as something that overflows from within artists; good art is a reflection of the imagination of the creator. As such, this book isn't a book about Christian art, necessarily, but about the cultivation of a Christian imagination from which beauty comes. Maritain draws on Augustine's notion to "love God and do what you want." Likewise, for the artist, Maritain suggests that the unique role of good artists is to "Cling to your creative intuition, and do what you want."[7] If we love God rightly, then our work will flow out of that love. In a similar way, if we see with a sacramental imagination, or a creative intuition, then our work will flow out of that love. Cling to your sacramental vision, and create what you want.

Before we get to outlining what a sacramental vision entails, we need to do some historical background of how we ended up with weak eyes that blur God's action in the world. Chapter 1 describes the first of these cataracts in rationalism. In the elevation of human potential, everything became explainable, and mystery has become limited to smaller and smaller pieces of God's creation. The second chapter outlines the vision impairment that is strict spiritualism. If rationalism elevated the material in the absence of spiritual presence, spiritualism denies the importance of the material. In essence, what is there doesn't really matter; what matters is the meaning we assign to it. By clearing out some of the dirt from our eyes, chapter 3 then presents how sacramentalism incorporates both material and spiritual for a clear, holistic vision. In many ways, this chapter "defines the term" of what we mean by a sacramental imagination. Whereas the habit of the materialist is to ignore the spiritual and the habit of the spiritualist to ignore the material, we want to suggest that it is by diving deeper into the material that we find the spiritual. Chapter 4 applies the sacramental vision specifically to artists in the ways they see the world and the work they create.

Chapter 5 further develops the concept of sacramental vision by discussing the concept of allegory and symbolism. By cultivating a sacred biblical imagination where we look for Christ in the Bible, as we raise our eyes

6. Maritain, *Creative Intuition*, 69.

7. Maritain, *Creative Intuition*, 45.

from the book up the world, we are more prone to see Christ in the creation. The world shines with creative energy and symbolic meaning as we are apprenticed in sacramental ways of seeing. The world becomes porous. To portray meaning in the world, chapter 6 describes the concepts of reserve and mystery. Just as Jesus told parables, artists communicate important truths that reveal subtle, sometimes hidden, realities. At times, preparation is needed to see correctly, and morality affects rational knowing.

The final chapter focuses on church participation. What can artists expect from the church in the formation of a sacramental imagination? It is our contention that the church is not an addendum to the Christian artist but central. Through liturgical and sacramental participation, the artist finds a place to slow down, contemplate, and reorder their desires. The community is necessary for a proper orientation to the world.

The bones of the books are as discussed above. But to put flesh on these ideas, we interspersed short vignettes between most chapters. These mini-chapters will take a concept from the previous chapter or two and offer a short, practical example. Some are pastoral reflections, others are contemplations of practicing artists, still others are historical examples. By weaving in these meditations, we want to offer artists examples of what the theory looks like in practice. In so doing, we hope not to say "this is the way to do it" but to spur on generative ideas in the life of artists.

At our core, we want to inspire courage in artists: the courage to see God in your material, the courage to harmonize your faith and artwork rather than to leave one or the other at the studio door, and the courage to help the church see God in new and different ways. As G. K. Chesterton referenced in the epigraph of this introduction, God, like a child, says to his creation, "Do it again!" And as artists with eyes to see, we can help display God's playfulness in his creation. With a sacramental vision, creators have the privileged position to show what the Creator is up to in his created world. With Reverend Ames, we want to see the same thing but with new eyes—the world shining like transfiguration.

As such, we should always be amateurs, which literally means "lovers." And our role as lovers is to "look the world back to grace."[8] We love that description that Robert Farrar Capon applies to chefs, and we think it applies just as well to artists. "Looking the world back to grace." If this is our task, we must love the world in such a way that we see God in it. And seeing God in the world affects the way we do our work as artists of love.

---

8. Capon, *Supper of the Lamb*, 19.

1

Easy Materialism: Reducing Reality

There is a need of an imaginative response to life, a training of the imagination, not merely in a few cases of poetic talent, but as a common function in every member of society. Incalculable harm can be done to men generally by the perversion or deadening of this faculty. When society becomes entirely secular and mechanized, men's common experience and imaginative furniture becomes secular. Divorced from nature and from a common religious experience, their minds are furnished with a stream of secular images and symbols. As the sensations flow on, the spiritual, creative forces of intellect and will are dulled. Men thus become more easily carried along in the stream of a mechanized external life.

—Conrad Pepler, *Riches Despised*

According to the earliest statements of Christian belief, redemption is not a process of making matter irrelevant but rather of making it permanent.

—Benjamin Myers, *Poetics of Orthodoxy*

What is art? It's a basic question but a complex one in the modern age. Does art have a form? Must art represent something? Or is art whatever the artist says it is? Must art serve a function, or is it merely form? These are important philosophical questions, but the authors are not philosophers. We're pastors and theologians and artists. So, let us simplify the task. We want to talk about what art does more than what art is, and a central premise of this book is that there is such a thing as good art and bad art. In the category of good art, we understand a broad sense and a narrow sense.

In the broad sense, good art provokes inner reflection and contemplation. Good art draws something out of us and draws us into the work. It decenters us. Good art is compelling, revelatory. Historically, this broad sense of art is affected by a recent adaptation that comes with the loss of meaning. With no objective meaning, meaning is what we impose. There is no divine order, no unquestionable meaning—only subjective interpretation. Reflecting on these developments Hans Jung asks in his *Art and the Question of Meaning*, "Can the work of art still be meaningful when the great synthesis of meaning no longer exists?"[1] In this world, the work of the artist is to "create and express new spiritual perceptions which we are all invited to share."[2] Into this modern world, Christian artists often feel hindered by explicit confessional commitments but have the opportunity to rightly display the human condition and invite viewers to contemplate something implicitly informed by Christian perception. One may call this a "quasi-sacramental" art.[3] The art inspires something, pulls something out of us, draws us in, but we're still functioning on the horizontal axis—an axis of individual interpretation and meaning.

In the narrow sense, good art is that which does not merely draw something out of us but draws us higher. Sacramental artists draw us out to draw us up, like the sacraments. The material form does not diminish a deeper meaning. The material form that artists create ties them back to the Lord of all matter. Junius Johnson suggests that this is why human artistry is never *ex nihilo*: "bread and wine, though human creations, still have obediential potency to God. God is the Lord not just of wheat and grapes but also bread and wine."[4] In other words, an artist's creation connects them back to the creative God. The material forms that artists develop have the potentiality to draw viewers back to the divine maker. It's in the eating, in the consumption, in the viewing of art that participants can be drawn into the life of God. Good artists connect viewers to their source, and if we attempt to be sacramental artists, that source is God. We hope to inspire in this narrow sense of good art, while appreciating and not diminishing the broad sense.

1. Küng, *Art and the Question of Meaning*, 31.

2. Howes, *Art of the Sacred*, 27.

3. We borrow this term with a slightly limited meaning from Junius Johnson in his *Father of Lights*, 146–58.

4. Johnson, *Father of Lights*, 162.

By positing such a thing as "good art" or "good taste," we don't mean to be elitist. Taste is not a matter of status or privilege. Rather, the cultivation of taste is a key means by which we disciple our passions. Not every initial impression is the correct one—for good or ill. Perhaps we approach a painting and think it's terrible; but then someone comes along and helps us see what at once we could not. They're training our taste, and thus vision. True beauty draws attention away from the tyranny of our own passions. The training of taste is an egalitarian affair.

But we may be getting ahead of myself. Before we describe what good, sacramental art is and what it inspires, we need to place ourselves in the modern art world. How did we get here? Why do so many feel this separation between their art and their faith? Why does art feel disconnected from the religious world? Why do many feel, as Makato Fujimura describes, like "border stalkers"—between two worlds of art and faith but never at home in either?[5] This and the next chapter attempt to describe the feel of our modern dysfunction.

MODERNITY AND RATIONALISM

"But the concept of health is rooted in the concept of wholeness. To be healthy is to be whole,"[6] writes Wendell Berry in *The Unsettling of America*. Aimed at a very different context (namely, agriculture in America), Berry highlights the distinctiveness of health as wholeness. But modernity and the industrial revolution has aimed at specialization and, therefore, fragmentation. Rather than seeing the whole, the modern world is prone to fracture into parts.

On second thought, arts and agriculture aren't too different. "Arts" often has a common noun attached to it: arts and culture. Berry's book has a noun attached to it, as well: culture and agriculture. Both agriculture and the arts deal with culture. And the culture in which we find ourselves seems divided and lacking wholeness (and therefore health).

Elsewhere, Berry argues the following: "I have been talking, of course, about a dualism that manifests itself in several ways: as a cleavage, a radical discontinuity, between Creator and creature, spirit and matter, religion and nature, religion and economy, worship and work, and so on. This dualism, I think, is the most destructive disease that afflicts us. In its best-known,

5. Fujimura, *Culture Care*, 58.
6. Berry, *Unsettling of America*, 103.

its most dangerous, and perhaps its fundamental version, it is the dualism of body and soul."[7] This dualism afflicts everyone in the modern age, and Christians aren't immune from the disease. In some profound ways, we contribute to the continued dualism of valuing soul over body, spirit over matter, worship over work. This disease runs deep.

The genesis of modern dualism can be traced back to the ancient theology of Gnosticism. In the gnostic heresy of the first century, there were two eternal forces: good and evil. Good existed in the soul, evil existed in the body. The goal was to shed the body's influence to unearth the pure soul. As a result, material existence—things like creation, nature, art—were shunned in favor of spirituality, soul, and interiority.

This interiority comes to its fullness in the Enlightenment. The philosopher Rene Descartes had an epistemological crisis. How could he know anything? How could he know that his reality wasn't a dream state? In his existential crisis, he went to his room to think. And in thinking, he found his answer. He knew he existed because he was thinking. Thus, his famous phrase, "I think, therefore I am." The material world could be a dream state, but one's thought life is so real, so right, so true, that it can't be denied. Thus, the creation is not endowed with inherent meaning or purpose, but its meaning and purpose are found in what I (or you) assign to it.

Following Descartes, the story of modernity unfolds. Reason is untouched by sin or error; reason is purity. Imagination, on the other hand, is a childish thing, something untrustworthy. There is no end or purpose of creation to be discovered; rather, meaning is assigned by mental study and experimentation. As Bill Nye the Science Guy exclaims, "Science rules." Creation is not a cosmos of meaning but a resource to extract by study. The world is a machine more than a living organism. We are alienated from the cosmos rather than belonging to it.

Owen Barfield notices this move as he writes, "Amid all the menacing signs that surround us in the middle of this twentieth century, perhaps the one which fills thoughtful people with the greatest sense of foreboding is the growing sense of meaninglessness. It is this which underlies most of the other threats."[8] When the world becomes a thing to manipulate or exploit, the world is robbed of meaning. In a quest for harmony with the external world, we've retreated to our mind, and thus, distanced ourselves from the world we sought to know and the meaning therein.

---

7. Berry, *Sex, Economy, Freedom and Community*, 104.

8. Barfield, *Rediscovery of Meaning and Other Essays*, 11.

Charles Taylor labels this interior turn in the religious life as excarnation. He describes excarnation as "a transfer out of embodied, 'enfleshed' forms of religious life, to those more 'in the head.' It follows in parallel with 'Enlightenment,' and modern unbelieving culture in general."[9] We live from our heads now more than our bodies. Modernity rid the world of magic in some true ways. Sea monsters don't exist in the waters and fairies don't exist in the forest. However, the scientific turn also unintentionally rid the world of God. When religion becomes a matter of thinking true things, then religion loses its embodied significance. Enfleshed forms of religious life through practice are less important than beliefs. We've retreated from the world of things and become confined to the mental world.

This move gave way to an understanding of human persons as "buffered." In Taylor's account, the medieval and premodern cosmos, creation was enchanted, rich with meaning. Human beings were porous, open to the divine. The modern self is buffered in the sense that it is closed off from the divine. The modern self is invulnerable and master of its own meanings. We have life between the moment we are born and the moment we die, but we inherit nothing before us and pass nothing on. In this "life under the sun," to use Ecclesiastes's parlance, we are left to find meaning, purpose, and identity all on our own. Depend on no one. Trust no institution. We're all individuals now.

In America, Robert Bellah and a group of researchers found that most citizens understand themselves in two ways: as utilitarian or expressive individuals.[10] We'll take up expressivism in the next chapter, but one can see how this modern buffer leads to utilitarian individualism. In essence, what has come to define American identity is whatever works. Pragmatism is our logic of choice. There is no meaning; there is only what works for us.

LITERAL INTERPRETATIONS

These briefly described developments would be lamentable to the larger culture if it weren't so entrenched in Christianity, as well. It's unsurprising to find rationalism or excarnation or utilitarianism in the church. Oftentimes, theology becomes an academic and cerebral activity, the embodied practices and postures are missing, and churches can tend to make

9. Taylor, *Secular Age*, 554.
10. See Bellah et al., *Habits of the Heart*, 32–33.

decisions based on whatever works. The problem is not merely "out there" but "in here."

The modern Protestant imagination, in particular, is smitten with the historical critical method of interpretation. In essence, this view of Scripture seeks the "literal sense," which means the historical circumstance and grammatical construction. The meaning lies in the words and in nothing more than the words or works they refer to. This method is a rationalistic and wooden way of interpreting Scripture (though an important and necessary method). We're not arguing that the literal does not matter; rather, we want to suggest deeper ways of reading Scripture and reading the world.

The theologian Hans Urs von Balthasar was one who saw these concerns and lamented the contemptible state of theology in the modern church. He wrote his systematic theology starting with beauty in his *Theological Aesthetics* before moving to reflections on goodness and truth. For Balthasar the journey to discussing the divine starts in the aesthetic experience, in beauty.[11] He argues that one way in which he sees the church losing its aesthetic and contemplative character is through the loss of Marian theology. (To be clear, we're gladly Protestant, though we sympathize

11. A key passage from Balthasar makes this clear: "It is not man's love for God that has set before itself an image of God so as to be able by this means to love God better: the image offers itself as something that could not have been invented by man—an image that can be read and understood and, therefore, believed only as an invention of God's love. The central question of so-called 'apologetics' or 'fundamental theology' is, thus, the question of perceiving form—an aesthetic problem. To have ignored this fact has stunted the growth of this branch of theology over the past hundred years. For fundamental theology, the heart of the matter should be the question, 'How does God's revelation confront man in history? How is it perceived?' But under the influence of a modern rationalistic concept of science, the question shifted ever more from its proper centre to the margin, to be re-stated in this manner: 'Here we encounter a man who claims to be God, and who, on the basis of this claim, demands that we should believe many truths he utters which cannot be verified by reason. What basis acceptable to reason can we give to his authoritative claims?' Anyone asking the question in this way has really already forfeited an answer, because he is at once enmeshed in an insoluble dilemma. On the one hand, he can believe on the basis of sufficient rational certainty; but then he is not believing on the basis of divine authority, and his faith is not Christian faith. Or, on the other hand, he can achieve faith by renouncing all rational certainty and believing on the basis of mere probability; but then his faith is not really rational. This is the kind of apologetics that distinguishes between a *content* to be believed which remains opaque to reason and the *'signs'* that plead for the rightness of this content, signs which, alas, prove either too much or too little." See Balthasar, *Glory of the Lord*, 167–68. He goes on to suggest aesthetic contemplation as being the primary method and means of theology.

with Balthasar's worry about the abandonment of Mary in Reformational churches).[12] Balthasar writes,

> Here the world is becoming imageless and valueless; it is a heap of "facts" which no longer say anything and in which an equally imageless and formless naked existence is freezing and anguishing in death. The philosophy and the theology of the image stand and fall together, and when the *image* of woman has vanished from the theological realm, an exclusively masculine, imagless conceptuality and thought-technique takes over, and then faith finds itself banished from the world and confined to the realm of the paradoxical and the absurd.[13]

Here, Balthasar is not arguing for the feminine at the expense or in competition with the masculine. Rather, he suggests that the feminine and the masculine need to be held together, reason and imagination in union.

Balthasar goes on to point out the excarnation that results in the denial of the incarnation. Christianity becomes disembodied when it's exclusively a heady exercise. Balthasar is, again, worth quoting:

> But, even if these images derive their symbolic language for man from the creation, in which God instructs man through essential images, nevertheless the correspondence between water and redemption, between oil and the Holy Spirit, between the laying on of hands and the conferring of the Spirit, derives its fittingness wholly from above, as instituted by the love of Christ, and this is shown even by the choice of images . . . they always need our experiential sensibility to direct them upwards into the sphere of the experience of faith.[14]

As Balthasar explains, the material takes on spiritual meaning when taken up in the language of God. Meaning becomes incarnated in physical forms, which expands and enhances the material through symbolic imagery.

For many, if something is literal then that means it doesn't have a deeper meaning. It just is what it is. The poet Malcolm Guite notices this loss of meaning and mystery in the modern world. He writes, "Scriptures were being read less as inspired poetry and more as the clock-maker's manual. It fell to poets, caught between these two blinkered rationalisms,

---

12. Milliner, *Mother of the Lamb*.

13. Balthasar, *Glory of the Lord*, 412.

14. Balthasar, *Glory of the Lord*, 413.

to preserve and develop the power inherent in language to mean more than one thing."[15] Scriptures are often read like an instruction manual of use or knowledge rather than a sacred text. So, as in the modern reading, we tend to explain the Word of God more than we meditate on it, contemplate it, or absorb it. But as Scripture is read to find what's true (rationalistic) or what to apply (utilitarian), then as our eyes turn up from the world of Scripture to the world of creation; the imagination affects our vision. We try to discern what's *really* true and what *really* works. We don't look for Christ or symbols. Our heads, rather than our bodies or affections, are the main interaction with the world. Embodiment, care, and affection are seen to get in the way of the "objective" truth-seeking. The mind matters over matter.

Or to use a sentence from Marilynne Robinson, "It is a triumph of science to have, in some degree, described the electron, and preposterous to suggest it has been explained."[16] In the same way, it is a triumph of the historical-critical method or the literal interpretation to describe Scripture, but preposterous to suggest that Scripture has been explained. There's a superabundance to Scripture just as there is a superabundance to beautiful art. There is more there than meets the eye, more there than the material, more there than words. Mystery lies in and through and beyond the material.

LITERAL ART

The way we interpret Scripture changes our perception and imagination of the world. When the church fathers looked up from interpreting Scripture in symbolical or metaphorical ways, they saw the world in symbolical and metaphorical ways. Their studying of Scripture impacted their study of the world. Modern interpretation methods impact the way we see the world. These developments impact the art world in several ways. In the broader world, as well as the Christian world, art is reduced to its pragmatic function, or our own understanding, which leads the way to a form of propaganda.

First, the modern art world is marked by the phrase "form follows function." Art is pragmatic more than it is meaningful. Particularly relevant in architecture, the structure of a building served the function of the building. The architecture was not about the dignity of humanity or beauty but

15. Guite, *Faith, Hope and Poetry*, 104.

16. Robinson, *Givenness of Things*, 22.

about how well it housed its inhabitants. An office building is for cubicles, a post office is for mail, and a train station is to get from A to B as efficiently and cleanly as possible. This development left our world stained with drab and ugly architecture. Likewise, in the art world, art can be seen as the bearer of a message that fits best. Good art is to be judged by what purpose it serves.

A fitting example of a style of art that reduces the reality of art is formalism. Formalism focuses on the lines or shapes for a judgment of beauty. Emotion comes from the form. These artists aren't concerned with emotions that we experience in life or with the context of an artist; rather, they produce and judge art solely on composition, only the visual components. They do not convey anything or represent anything; they merely focus on shapes. Art is reduced to the medium and ignores the context. At its most extreme, everything one needs to know is in the work of art itself. There is nothing more.

Second, in our material world, art can be reduced to its ideas and our understanding. Art is a mere carrier of cognition. In this way, art isn't concerned with beauty as much as it is with truth. Much historical reflection on beauty falls prey to a sort of materialism. Art is representation or imitation. In an earlier iteration, Aquinas qualified good art by its proportion, wholeness, and radiance. These characteristics depicted the "splendor of truth" and beauty needed thought. Beauty is more cerebral than sensational. In Aquinas's threefold distinction, they all have to do with the material image. Ultimately, beauty is found in the form and content of the painting. Does it exhibit harmony or balance? Is it full or is something missing? These are all adequate and important questions to get at beauty but it tends to the rationalistic, like we're going through an image with a checklist, marking off the three qualifications. Yet how do you measure something like radiance? It gets at something important but it doesn't quite mark the material object. There's something superabundant about it. Aquinas will have more to say on beauty, but if we take his classic threefold approach as popularly quoted, it can be cognitively reductive.

In a later iteration, particularly before the invention of the camera, art was judged by how well it represented its subject. Good artists were those who could draw or paint or sculpt closest to (what would later be known as) the photographic representative. Some still judge an artist by his or her ability to proportionally and harmoniously represent a "pure" image. Good art isn't in interpretation or perspective but in realism. In all of these representations, the form or content remains king, and art is judged by how well it conveys its message.

Commenting on the dialogue following Plato, Etienne Gilson argues, "the Western philosophical tradition always remained faithful to this attitude which reduces art to knowledge and makes of man-made beauty a variety of truth."[17] Gilson is commenting on the idea from Plato that art is imitation, so why make a shadow when you can contemplate the Ideal Form in the intellectual and divine world? Plato never regarded art very highly, and his reflections on beauty were sometimes reductive in this stream of thought. Gilson goes on to say that in the Platonian world, art would be banished except for civic propaganda and moral education.[18]

By and large, Gilson's warning is Christian art's prevailing presence. Christians often use art as propaganda and moral education. Connecting scriptural vision with artistic vision, Graham Howes contends, "as the interpretation of Scripture became increasingly questioned, and the historical Jesus partly demythologised (especially by German scholarship), so painters of religious themes sought—at times quite consciously—to sustain Christian morale by underlining the visual authenticity of the settings for Bible narrative, even if the literal truth of the narrative itself was being increasingly treated with scholarly skepticism. They also sold more paintings that way."[19] As such, Christian art became a type of apologetic or propaganda, teaching the faithful what to believe. Art is not for contemplation but for didactic lessons, reducing art to pithy teaching or summary subjects.

Thus, what qualifies as good or beautiful art is biblical scenes. Or, in a more extreme prohibition used by J. I. Packer, beckoning the Deuteronomic proscription[20] to not make idols, art can only be scriptural words and verses.[21] As such, beauty is disincarnated or excarnated. Packer goes on to say this is why we should close our eyes in prayer, so that no mental image is mistaken for the image of God. Art, in many respects, is seen to be idolatrous. Again, theology starts in mental understanding more than aesthetic contemplation, exemplifying Balthasar's critique of Protestant theology.

17. Gilson, *Arts of the Beautiful*, 114.

18. Gilson, *Arts of the Beautiful*, 120.

19. Howes, *Art of the Sacred*, 41.

20. See Deuteronomy 4–5.

21. Packer, *Knowing God*, 47–50.

Furthermore, art can be seen as a distraction from justice in the world, at best, or a distraction from salvation, at worst. Calvin Seerveld illustrates this tendency in *Rainbows in a Fallen World*. He argues that many "have largely swallowed the technocratic tyranny of our culture whole, which means that we live by economized control—efficiency."[22] There's no time for enjoyment or contemplation when there are things to get done. Seerveld goes on to discuss an obedient aesthetic life. An aesthetic life is not a matter of salvation, but it is one of obedience; a disobedient aesthetic life is one deprived of beauty and pleasure. He gives the example of using Styrofoam cups and lawn chairs and a folding table for dinner. For some, that's the best they can do. But if we were to eat every meal with meager and disposable containers, there would be some element missing from life, some superabundance. These practical elements do "the job" yet there's something about Christianity that encourages a deeper and more intimate relationship in our aesthetic life. We are people of the resurrection, and therefore of abundance and joy. In something as simple and mundane as dining utensils, we are invited to celebrate by living obediently.

Even Jesus' first miracle was an example of this celebratory overflow. At the wedding feast at Cana, Jesus did not merely meet needs by supplying water or meet desires by providing wine that would suffice. He produced an abundance of fine wine. Jesus is lavish with his creation, and invites us, as his followers, to think abundantly in our aesthetic life. As Wendell Berry poetically puts it, we ought to do things that don't compute. Plant sequoias. Buy things that aren't merely useful or pragmatic but beautiful.[23]

CONCLUSION

In an essay entitled "The Nature and Aim of Fiction," Flannery O'Connor describes the three senses of Scripture found in medieval interpretations: allegorical, tropological, and anagogical. All these meanings were based on the literal meaning, what we could call the material meaning of a text. She encourages writers to develop an anagogical seeing, which is a kind of vision that is "able to see different levels of reality in one image or situation."[24]

22. Seerveld, *Rainbows for a Fallen World*, 61.

23. As quoted in his poem, "Manifesto: The Mad Farmer Liberation Front," in *Mad Farmer Poems*, 18.

24. O'Connor, *Mystery and Manners*, 72. The full context is as follows: "The kind of vision the fiction writer needs to have or to develop, in order to increase the meaning

This attitude toward Scripture is also an attitude toward life and toward art. Just as a good poem can never be reduced to its mere words, so good visual art can never be reduced to the material form or its explanation. Rather, "the whole story is the meaning because it is an experience, not an abstraction."[25] If we can riff off O'Connor, the whole picture is the meaning, because it is an aesthetic experience, not an abstraction.

The mere materialism is not to ignore the material, but to see more than the material, to encounter mystery, abundance, and beauty. For this to occur, artists need to cultivate an anagogical vision, which we call sacramental. However, before we prescribe the corrective lenses, we also need to detect another distortion of sight. There are always at least two ways to fall off the road. One is to focus too much on cognition and pragmatics and material. The other is to ignore the material altogether to get to the spiritual meaning. This chapter focused on reducing reality. The next chapter will focus on ignoring or overlooking physical reality in favor of the spiritual.

of his story is called anagogical vision, and that is the kind of vision that is able to see different levels of reality in one image or one situation."

25. O'Connor, *Mystery and Manners*, 73.

2

Cheap Spirituality: Overlooking Reality

So it is that Christian art today is caught between two fires (as perhaps it always has been): it must oppose the cult of the ugly, which says that everything beautiful is a deception and only the representation of what is crude, low and vulgar is the truth, the true illumination of knowledge. Or it has to counter the deceptive beauty that makes the human being seem diminished instead of making him great, and for this reason is false.

—Pope Benedict

THE STORY OF MODERNITY is a story ridding the world of mystery, and with mystery, the divine. The world has been divided between soul and body, faith and science, church and academy, worship and work. The latter of those pairs wins out. We are the proverbial material girls in a material world. Everything can be observed, examined, and subsequently, explained. As seen in the last chapter, art becomes a blend of pragmaticism and materialism with a dash of propaganda or moral education thrown in.

This divide has ancient roots. In the gnostic heresy, the divide rejected the body in favor of the spiritual. In the modern divide, the material was accepted in rejection of the spiritual. In the postmodern divide, the spiritual comes back with a vengeance. Embodiment is ignored altogether. In the modern age, the tendency was to ignore symbolism to impose or create meaning by oneself. In the postmodern age, everything is a symbol to be freely interpreted by the individual. In the modern age, meaning was stable and available to be discoverable in a joint enterprise. In a postmodern age, meaning is mine alone.

THE RISE OF THE SPIRITUAL SELF

The story of postmodernity has been told in different ways at different times. To be clear, what follows is not an intellectual history or philosophy lesson. Rather, we paint with broad strokes about particular players, which develops an ethos or feel about an exclusive spirituality. Philip Reiff calls the rise of an identity rooted in internal understandings the triumph of therapeutic culture.[1] For Rieff, with the loss of shared moral meaning, the self becomes sacred. Since every self is sacred, there are no objective truths but subjective interpretations, any one of which is no better or worse than others.

James Nolan Jr. helpfully defines the therapeutic under these five points:

(1) a pronounced cultural preoccupation with the individual self,

(2) a notable concern with the place of emotions in making sense of oneself and one's place in the world,

(3) the emergence of a new class of counselors, psychologists, and therapists who have been socially recognized as those most qualified to guide the emotion-laden self through the complexities of modern social life,

(4) the reinterpretation of a growing number of behaviors through the pathologically determined heuristic of addiction, disorder, and dysfunction, and

(5) the unique cultural salience of the "language of victimhood."[2]

The therapeutic concoction leads to personal identity as being fragile, needing constant affirmation, and requiring more recognition and support from popular opinion, as described by Charles Taylor in *The Malaise of Modernity*.[3] In such a world, there are no ideals, only choices. There are no obligations or attachments, only self-determination.

Mark Edmundson describes this therapeutic move in *Self and Soul*. He takes an intellectual history tour through literature to highlight the shift from the ancient understanding of the soul to the perception of the modern

---

1. Reiff, *Triumph of the Therapeutic.*

2. As defined by Lasch-Quinn, "Ancient Philosophy's Return Amidst the Triumph of the Therapeutic." Also see Nolan Jr., *Therapeutic Self.*

3. Taylor, *Malaise of Modernity.*

self. The soul is relational, filled with meaning, while the self is individual. For the self, appetites are to be ceded to, whereas, with the conception of the soul, appetites are to be reigned in and controlled. When self reigns supreme, ideals wane, since there are no common goals but only individual perspectives. And "without ideals, life lacks significant meaning."[4] There is nothing higher than the self, and therefore, all have to answer to each individual monad. It's no wonder meaning, significance, and purpose are the most talked about issues for young people today. All they have is themselves to figure it out in supposedly the only unique, authentic path available to them.

So, as Robert Bellah highlights in *Habits of Heart*, what emerges is a self-identity that his research group termed expressive individualism. Summarizing much of the ideas and thoughts from the above interlocutors, Bellah and his group describe expressive individuals this way:

> The right act is simply the one that yields the agent the most exciting challenge or the most good feeling about himself. Now if selves are defined by their preferences, but those preferences are arbitrary, then each self constitutes its own moral universe, and there is finally no way to reconcile conflicting claims about what is good in itself . . . All we can appeal to in relationships with others is their self-interest, likewise enlightened, or their intuitive sympathies . . . In the absence of any objectifiable criteria of right and wrong, good or evil, the self and its feelings become our only moral guide.[5]

These sentiments seem as natural as the air we breathe. It's what we inherit by living in the contemporary world. But this normal developed from somewhere. In the premodern world, the divine was the center of the universe. In the modern world, truth or rationality determined thought and action. But in the postmodern world, the self becomes central. Although it seems like the water we swim in, this story has important philosophical underpinnings in recent history.

The roots of feelings as a moral guide have roots that extend into the eighteenth century with the philosopher David Hume. These understandings of the self come with an epistemological turn, as well. As Hume is famously quoted, "Reason is, and ought only to be the slave of the passions,

---

4. Edmundson, *Self and Soul*, 102.
5. Bellah et al., *Habits of the Heart*, 76.

and can never pretend to any other office than to serve and obey them."[6] Therefore, ethics is based on emotion rather than principles or ideals. We offer reasons as justifications for what the passions want, and the passions lead the way. Rather than a strict logic as seen last chapter, the emerging reaction is strict emotivism. As such, Hume is known as a sentimentalist (which will have important implications when discussing sentimental art).

Likewise, Hume's ethical philosophy is rooted in the belief that we only have what is, so we can never say what ought to be. This thought led to Lawrence Kholberg's moral theory of development, wherein humans don't aim at a certain morality or moral code or principles; rather, they are placed by which stage they are in. (There are no moral judgments, just evaluations.) All that we have is what is. There are no oughts to be conformed to or ideals to pursue. All we do is develop . . . toward nothing in particular.[7] The roots of Hume grew into the tree of postmodernism in the likes of Jean Sartre, who claimed that man shows up and then defines himself. There is no fundamental nature or common vision for others. The individual chooses and self-creates.[8] This development toward nothing accounts for some of art drawing out but not drawing up. Art is seen to be provocative in picturing something but since there are no oughts, art is ready made. It's our ideas which frame what art is.

That may be some (brief) philosophical heavy lifting, but we highlight all these perspectives of identity because these epistemic roots bleed into postmodern or spiritualist art. But before we see these philosophical developments take root, we also want to show the way Christian subculture encourages this postmodern vision with our own language, as well.

THE SEARCH FOR THE SPIRITUAL MEANING

At the turn of the nineteenth century, scholars initiated a quest for the historical Jesus. In their view, there was a discrepancy between the historical Jesus and the Christ of faith.

In other words, the "real" Jesus and the "spiritual" Jesus were in conflict and needed some ironing out. Perhaps the historical Jesus did not exist at all. But we could still learn spiritual lessons. Modern man had difficulty accepting the miraculous parts of the Bible, so Christianity needed

6. Hume, *Treatise of Human Nature*, 3.3.3.

7. See Kohlberg and Mayer, "Development as the Aim of Education."

8. See Sartre, *Existentialism Is a Humanism*.

a facelift. We needed a modern Christianity for the modern man. Gnosticism, separating material and spiritual, reared its ugly head again. While those on the more conservative end of the spectrum may desire to prove the Bible literally true, those on the more liberal end attempt to vacate the literal completely. Rather, the meaning is found in its sentiments, in what we make of it. Did the exodus really need to happen to teach about God's saving power against injustice? Perhaps it can be read as merely a spiritual lesson. Modern man knows that man cannot materially rise from the dead, so the Christ of faith taught that God can make metaphorical dead things come alive. The truth is found in the spiritual understanding, not in the material matters.

While we assume many readers may not be sympathetic to the quest for the historical Jesus, our interpretative vision is also disordered. Alister McGrath suggests that Gnosticism appeals to contemporary taste by interpreting "Christianity as a religion of self-discovery, not redemption. Religion is the quest for true inner identity, the 'real me,' the inner spark of divine life, or the gold in the mud."[9] Christianity becomes a means to my best life now. God is not the center; I am. The philosophy of the spiritual self takes root in our Christian vision, so we adapt the modern story to make sense of a spiritualized Christianity. We are too blessed to be stressed. Any time the gnostic heresy takes root, we have faith detached from creation, and especially from the fall.

Furthermore, in the modern age, perhaps the stereotypical hermeneutic was the question, "What is true?" and "How's this apply?" In the postmodern age, the hermeneutical question turns to "What's this mean to me?" or "How does this make you feel?" The individual becomes the sole interpreter. A central premise of this book is that the main questions we ask of the Bible direct and influence our vision of creation, and therefore, of artistic creation. Rather than let a biblical and sacramental vision inform our imagination, modern stories often direct our gaze.

CHEAP ART

A major change in the art world came with the invention of the photograph. In a bygone era, artists painted portraits or a rolling countryside or famous historical scenes. Leonardo da Vinci was known for the intense, realistic detail he brought to his artwork. However, with the photograph, their work

9. McGrath, *Heresy*, 232.

was replaced. Why pay someone to paint when a more accurate representation could be had with the click of a button? (Or, we suppose at this time, the pull of a cord.) So, the art world adapted. Representation was not the purpose of art. A precursor to these changing tides were the Impressionists, who weren't painting in order to get an exact representation but to capture the mood of a particular moment.

In the contemporary art world, the mood of artists runs the show. Marcel Duchamp provoked a revolution of art with his infamous *Fountain*. In artistic fame, he bought a urinal, wrote "R Mutt 1917" on it, turned it sideways, and presto: it's an art piece. As art historian Will Gompertz notes, Duchamp created a new art form: "one where an artist could select any pre-existing mass-produced object with no obvious aesthetic merit, and by freeing it from its functional purpose—in other words making it useless—and by giving it a name and changing the context and angle from which it would normally be seen, turn it into a de facto artwork."[10] Duchamp called it "ready-made" art. This idea of art became preeminent. Art wasn't so much made "by" an artist as it was "from" an artist. Gompertz goes on to describe the previous era when "the medium always came first, and only then would an artist be allowed to project his or her ideas on to a painting, sculpting or drawing." After *The Fountain*, the process got turned around. "(Duchamp) considered the medium to be secondary: first and foremost was the idea."[11] We saw last chapter that a mark of modern art was that form follows function. In the contemporary art world, form follows idea. In other words, the point of art becomes the communication of an idea rather than the apprehension of beauty.

One example of form following idea is conceptual art. Typically, conceptual art emphasizes an idea over a style, as argued by Anthony Janson: "with conceptual artists, idea, concept, or information will be the consuming quality of the work,"[12] or as Elizabeth Schellekens puts it, "for most conceptual artists, artistic value is only to be gained from the knowledge, insight, or understanding that artworks may generate."[13] The idea is all-important; form is legion. It's a reversal of traditional art definitions where the craft or form is central. One can see Duchamp's *Fountain* as the precursor and foundation of conceptual art. He had an idea, and he

10. Gompertz, *What Are You Looking At?*, 4.

11. Gompertz, *What Are You Looking At?*, 6.

12. Davies et al., eds., *Janson's History of Art*, 1062.

13. Schellekens, *Aesthetic Value of Ideas*, 80.

used art to turn his idea over to a medium or craft, but it didn't start with the craft. Commenting on this turn in art, Will Gompertz comments, "An artist's job was not to give aesthetic pleasure—designers could do that; it was to step back from the world and attempt to make sense or comment on it through the presentation of ideas that had no functional purpose other than themselves."[14] Medium is secondary, idea was primary. Art is consumed in the idea. Art, then, is like an object lesson. It doesn't draw us in by the material but pulls us inward to reflect on our own consciousness. Art becomes an expression of the artist and a reflection of the person consuming it. So, when I see a biblical picture, I find it beautiful, because I know the story of Moses. It's not adding new knowledge or taking me deeper into an understanding; I'm reflecting on what I already know. To be fair, there is value in conceptual art; good art does cause a deeper reflection. Good art does communicate ideas in a profoundly aesthetic way that mere words could not. However, if communication is all art can do, then it's just downstream of expressive individualism. It's no wonder why conceptual art is popular in the postmodern art world.

As the secular age continues, as Charles Taylor notices, art as imitation turns to art as *poiesis*.[15] In other words, art imitating nature turns to art making its own world. The artist creates his or her own world rather than representing anything concrete. Abstract art is tempted in the same way. Commenting on "suprematism," Kazamir Malevish notes, "The happy liberating touch of nonobjectivity drew me out into the 'desert' where only feeling is real . . . From the suprematist point of view, the appearances of natural objects are in themselves meaningless; the essential thing is feeling—in itself and completely independent of the context in which it has been evoked."[16] Feelings take center stage in abstract art, away from material reality.

The postmodern world also breeds a sort of individuality and expressivity that encourages a loner mentality. The motif becomes one of the individual genius, who may be at differing levels crazy. Artists like Vincent van Gogh in the visual art world or the ideal expressive individualist Walt Whitman[17] in the poetic world become certain exemplars of what a great artist is.

---

14. Gompertz, *What Are You Looking At?*, 10.

15. Taylor, *Secular Age*, 353–54.

16. Malevish, *Gegastandlose Welt*, 452–53, quoted in Maritain, *Creative Intution*, 148.

17. Robert Bellah describes Whitman's idealism as "a life rich in experience, open to

There are three consequences of the expressivist philosophy to the contemporary art world. Cheap spirituality encourages a sentimentality that overlooks reality, which leads to the popularization of kitsch art in both secular and Christian versions.

First, the art academy has its own form of snobbery or Gnosticism. So often, there is a "secret knowledge" that only the inside crowd or "elite" has access to. If you're getting into the art world, you may feel overwhelmed and ignorant. And there is a place for training and knowing what to look for and know what beauty is. However, it can often feel that judgment about a great work of art is reserved for some special elite (and especially the rich). It can seem like everyone looks at you and think, "Well, don't you see it?" If not, then you're not elite. No explanations. No reasons. Just expression from the artist, and if you don't get it, then you're not in the "in" crowd. Only those trained in art institutions can appreciate art. Only they understand the label "fine" in the "fine arts."

Second, a focus on the spiritual can lead to a sentimentality that ignores the realities of the world. In *A Peculiar Orthodoxy*, Jeremy Begbie describes three results of sentimentalism: it misrepresents reality by evading or trivializing evil, it is emotionally self-indulgent, and it avoids appropriate costly action.[18] Benjamin Myers defines sentimentality as "emotional satisfaction without emotional connection, an agreement between the artist and the audience to skip straight to the gratification, which, due to the skipping, is not so gratifying after all."[19] Continuing, Myers critiques the popular Christian artist Thomas Kinkade. In his artistic philosophy, Kinkade wanted to depict life without the fall, full of cozy little cottages and beautiful landscapes.[20] But Myers provocatively asks, "What is the warmth of home without knowing the coldness of the world? What is homecoming without the hard journey?"[21] He goes on: "Kinkade's error is not in

---

all kinds of people, luxuriating in the sensual as well as the intellectual, above all a life of strong feeling." Bellah et al., *Habits of the Heart*, 34.

18. Begbie, *Peculiar Orthodoxy*, 26–35.

19. Myers, *Poetics of Orthodoxy*, 41.

20. Flannery O'Connor responds to sentimentality by pointing out that "sentimentality is excess, a distortion of sentiment usually in the direction of an overemphasis on innocence, and that innocence, wherever it is overemphasized in the ordinary human condition. We lost our innocence in the Fall, and our return to it is through Redemption which was brought about by Christ's death and by our slow participation in it." O'Connor, *Mystery and Manners*, 148.

21. Myers, *Poetics of Orthodoxy*, 41.

depicting the homecoming; it is in ignoring the seeking. That is why, when a student recently told me that she lovingly sends a Kinkade postcard to her grandmother once a month, I blurted, 'Stop sending pornography to your grandma!' Art must be truthful in what it says about the world and our sojourn in it. Lying down in green pastures is a great goal for an artist, but he must not attempt to get there without walking through the valley of the shadow of death. If he does, he is a liar."[22] Good art cannot ignore the ugliness or reality of the world; it must incarnate to know it truly. Sentimentalism distorts what is true.[23]

Lastly, sentimentality leads to kitsch art. Kitsch is the result of Begbie's second distortion of sentimentality: emotional self-indulgence. In other words, kitsch art gives us feeling for feeling's sake. The satisfaction is having the emotion. Kitsch can be seen in the portrayal of both happiness and suffering alike, in a sappy song or a sad one. Sentimentalism tends to focus on emotion as a means to a false end, never leading us to reality. John Ruskin writes, "It is to confound admiration with hunger, love with lust, and life with sensation; it is to assert that the human creature has no ideas and no feelings, except those ultimately referable to its brutal appetites."[24] This form of sentimentality causes people to worship desire itself without actually acknowledging the object of ultimate desire. In the words of Calvin Seerveld, "Kitsch oversimplifies emotional nuances and reduces aesthetically sensitive life to a one-track, predictable, pseudo-transcendent satisfaction."[25] In all these ways, kitsch overlooks reality by delving into a false substitute.

Connecting the theme of kitsch to conceptional art, Hans-Georg Gadamer urges:

> There is the case when we enjoy something for the sake of some quality or other that is familiar to us. I think that this is the origin of kitsch and all bad art. Here we see only what we already know, not wishing to see anything else. We enjoy the encounter insofar as it simply provides a feeble confirmation of the familiar, instead of changing us. This means that the person who is already prepared for the language of art can sense the intention behind the effect. All kitsch has something of this forced quality about it.[26]

22. Myers, *Poetics of Orthodoxy*, 41.

23. For more on the evangelical tendency toward sentimentality, see Brenneman, *Homespun Gospel.*

24. Ruskin, *Modern Painters II*, 221.

25. Seerveld, *Rainbows for a Fallen World*, 66.

26. Gadamer, *Relevance of the Beautiful*, 52.

Again, all we have is inner reflection and art as an object lesson. Art, then, can only be familiar; art can never take us higher, because there is no higher. There is only what is. Or, as Seerveld suggests, "Kitsch never enlarges experience; it blandly affects a show to stimulate feelings of exquisiteness or a mood of supernal tenderness, but it flops into bathos simply because it is ersatz . . . Kitsch is like deodorant next to good perfume."[27] Kitsch is a cheap substitute for deep feeling, faux feeling that feels "authentic" but is manufactured, at best, or deceptive, at worst.

ENTERING THE REAL

In sum, sentimentalists want the emotion without the cost. So how does a Christian artist relate to the ugliness of the world? More to the point, is it possible that something that is ugly can actually be beautiful—are there ugly "types"? How do such possibilities affect artistic vision? One example of an answer is Grünewald's *Isenheim* altarpiece. It depicts the gruesome death and agony of the crucifixion but remains alluring in its beauty. Jesus is off-center, a ghoulish green color, stretched out in inhumane and disproportionate ways. Yet, there is something beautiful about the grotesque. It's revelatory in form and idea. This also holds true in the Pieta, the beauty of God revealed in the dead body of Jesus. Nancy Bedford states, "In Christ God assumes our suffering, not to glorify suffering in itself but to open the path to abundant life from its true solidarity with the worst things human beings can endure: suffering, torture, death, loss of loved ones."[28] It is true that one of the most beautiful events in history is the cross of Christ, whose form did not appear beautiful by earthly standards, but was a bold proclamation of absolute beauty. The crucifixion was always an offense to the senses. Paul proclaimed the cross to be a stumbling block in 1 Corinthians 1:23. In this way, Christians must confront worldly aesthetics, exhibiting that beauty is not always the way things appear, that absolute beauty pushes beyond the reflection of things as they are. If beauty is derived from the One that is Beauty, then we must not stop at prettiness, but to truthfully represent beauty as that which embraces the ugly truth of self-giving love. Hans Urs von Balthasar describes it this way: "[God's beauty] embraces the most abysmal ugliness of sin and hell by virtue of the condescension of divine love, which has brought even sin and hell into that divine art for

27. Seerveld, *Rainbows for a Fallen World*, 63.
28. Bedford, "Beauty of God," 46.

which there is no human analogue."[29] The cross, as the paradigm where love is most clearly shown, reorientates the Christian vision of beauty. It is the climax of love, and therefore, beauty. And there's nothing kitschy about it.

In the paradox of Christian vision, sometimes those acquainted with suffering and the grotesque are the best at seeing beauty. Commenting on the art that emerged out of World War II, Hans Feibusch comments,

> There is another danger . . . that of talking baby language. To see the way some of our best church and cathedral builders decorate their work with nursery emblems, golden stars, chubby Christmas angels, lilies, lambs and shepherds, insipid sculptures and paintings of a silly, false naivety, one wonders in what world they live. The men who came home from war, and all the rest of us, have seen too much horror and evil; when we close our eyes terrible sights haunt us; the world is seething with bestiality; and it is all man's doing. Only the most profound, tragic, moving, Sublime vision can redeem us. The voice of the Church should be heard above the thunderstorm; and the artist should be her mouthpiece.[30]

Those who have stared down evil and suffering and emerged transformed model Jesus, who did the same. This echoes Dionysius's discussion of ascent, and beauty's ability to draw our minds away from earthly passions. In so doing so, he is not suggesting we escape, but rather, we should find our highest meaning and purpose in who we are. Beauty calls us back to who we truly are—we find reality found not in escaping the created world. The Beauty that we witness does not draw us out of this world to a more ideal one, but to embrace the one in which we live. Creation, here and now, becomes more vibrant as we come to see it as it truly is in God.

29. Balthasar, *Glory of the Lord*, 124.

30. Feibusch, *Mural Painting*, 54–55, cited in Howes, *Art of the Sacred*, 71.

The "Integration" of Faith
and Art—David J.P. Hooker

IN 2005 I STARTED teaching at Wheaton College. It wasn't my first teaching gig; I had been both a professional artist and a committed Christian for more than a decade at that point, but it was the first time I was introduced to the world of Christian higher education. It didn't take very long before I encountered the "I" word: integration. While I had some thoughts about how my art and my faith interacted, suddenly there was a great sense of urgency to nail it down. I took a kind of self-guided crash course in art and theology. I had not realized how much really great work had been done in that area, and it continues to be a thriving subject in both church and academia. Even the really big names, it seemed, had written on the topic. Take these two examples.

The first is from Pope Benedict XVI's Address to Artists in 2009. "We need you," he said. "We need your collaboration in order to carry out our ministry . . . Authentic beauty . . . unlocks the yearning of the human heart, the profound desire to know, to love, to go towards the Other, to reach for the Beyond. There is a kind of incarnation of God in the world, of which beauty is the sign. Beauty is the experimental proof that incarnation is possible."

The second is from N. T. Wright's sermon "The Apocalyptic and the Beauty of God," in 2006.

> I was brought up in a world where the arts constituted, as it were, the pretty border around the edge of reality, . . . as more or less a way of sugaring the pill, of making the Bible listenable-to, not as something to be integrated more tightly within a Christian worldview. The vocation of the artist is to speak of the present as beautiful in itself but as pointing beyond itself, to enable us to see both the glory that already fills the earth and the glory that shall

flood it to overflowing; to speak, within that, of the shame without ignoring the promise, and to speak of the promise without forgetting the shame.

That is a lot to digest! When I come across words like this, I find I am both inspired and intimidated. Both of these church leaders are expressing the idea that art as a vehicle of transcendence: and that the artist's vocation is to express both beauty and brokenness, and "to call forth dreams and hopes," and "to reach for the Beyond."

This is an attractive vision for me as an artist in many ways. I want my artwork to be transcendent, to move people, to inspire. After all, I became an artist because I had an experience with artworks that were transcendent in ways much like both Pope Benedict XVI and N. T. Wright describe. I suspect everyone reading this who considers art-making a part of their vocation can say much the same thing. In my case, I can remember that first transcendent encounter with an artwork. It was with Louise Bourgeois's "Night Garden."

The challenge is that while I certainly aspire to create art that is transcendent, that can't be my starting point, or I'm doomed to failure before I even begin. The weight of that expectation is too much to bear. It leaves me paralyzed; unable to create. Or I may begin, but I'll be editing all the way through the process, and the work ends up lifeless, because I did not allow it to have free will. And in the end, I think transcendence is out of my control. Isn't that the work of the Holy Spirit? The best I can do is invite the Spirit in—to set the table, so to speak—and hope I recognize its presence.

The types of writing that I find helpful in approaching my practice comes mostly from other artists, particularly those who emphasize mystery and discovery as essential to the process of making. Here's a couple of examples.

Georgia O'Keefe:

> I feel that a real living form is the result of the individual's effort to create the living thing out of the adventure of his spirit into the unknown—where it has experienced something—felt something—it has not understood—and from that experience comes the desire to make the unknown—known. By unknown—I mean the thing that means so much to the person that wants to put it down—clarify something he feels but does not clearly understand—sometimes he partially knows why—sometimes he doesn't—sometimes it is all working in the dark—but a working that must be done—Making the unknown—known—in terms of

> one's medium is all-absorbing—if you stop to think of the form—
> as form you are lost—The artist's form must be inevitable—You
> mustn't even think you won't succeed—Whether you succeed or
> not is irrelevant—there is no such thing. Making your unknown
> known is the important thing—and keeping the unknown always
> beyond you—catching crystallizing your simpler clearer version
> of life—only to see it turn stale compared to what you vaguely feel
> ahead—that you must always keep working to grasp—the form
> must take care of itself if you can keep your vision clear.

And Ann Hamilton:

> One doesn't arrive—in words or in art—by necessarily knowing
> where one is going. In every work of art something appears that
> does not previously exist, and so, by default, you work from what
> you know to what you don't know. You may set out for New York,
> but you may find yourself, as I did, in Ohio. You may set out to
> make a sculpture and find that time is your material. You may pick
> up a paintbrush and find that your making is not on canvas or
> wood but in relations between people. You may set out to walk
> across the room, but getting to what is on the other side might take
> ten years. You have to be open to all possibilities and to all routes
> circuitous or otherwise.

While it is not an outright contradiction, there's a tension between setting out to make work that "speaks of the present as beautiful in itself, but as pointing beyond itself," as NT Wright put it, and "working from what you know to what you don't know," as Ann Hamilton put it. I may make work that fulfills both, but if I set out to do both, I'm going to get stuck.

While I enjoy reading and teaching at the intersection of art and theology, I must admit it is also a challenge. Writings on the topic, like much of art criticism, are mostly based on outcomes: they are answering the question, "What is art for?" While that is an important question, it is not the question that I can take with me everyday into the studio. I believe in art as a way of knowing: that is to say that the act of making creates much of the meaning. I tend towards ways of working that are primarily process and materials based. My art practice is less about making work that points in a particular direction, and more of an open-ended exploration. I see myself less as a prophet with a message to bring to the world, and more as a scientist with an impossible-to-prove hypothesis, mucking about with the materials, places, and experiences around me, and sharing my questions, my curiosities, and my sense of wonder with the world.

One of the ways I began to understand how my artwork and my faith were connected was by rereading the parables that Jesus taught. The parables in Matthew 13 have been a source of interest to me for some time. Perhaps it is because the idea of heaven is such a difficult one for me to grasp. Parables are, I think, about transcendence. While I'm no expert on parables, any time I approach them I am reminded of the wisdom given to me by Deacon Mary Baker: If you ever think you fully understand a parable, that's a sign that you don't. Bearing that in mind, here's a partial list of the ways Jesus describes the kingdom of heaven in the chapter. It's quite a diverse list of very ordinary things: a farmer gathering seed, a woman mixing yeast in bread dough, a net used by fishermen, to name a few. When I was younger and read these parables, I thought of them as always pointing up: the everyday things were there to point my gaze up towards the kingdom of heaven. But over time I have come to see that these parables not only help us look up to see heaven, they also bring heaven down to earth, helps us see it in the here and now. That is to say, transcendence has become a two-way street. The kingdom of heaven is manifest in ordinary things!

This insight has had profound impact on my thinking about how my art practice and my faith intersect. Maybe instead of always thinking that my work, if it is to be transcendent, must point people towards the mystery of God, I can think of it as showing how the mystery of God is already present in the small, ordinary things of daily life. Maybe the ordinary and the transcendent don't meet at an overlapping intersection, but rather there is a thin, porous membrane between the two. Making art becomes less an act of will or inspiration, or trying to reach out to the beyond, and instead, it becomes an act of noticing, of being patient, of practicing presence.

3

The Visible and Invisible: Toward a Sacramental Imagination

The sunlight in a picture is therefore not related to real sunlight simply as written words are to be spoken. It is a sign, but also something more than a sign, because in it the thing signified is really in a certain mode present. If I had to name the relation I should call it not symbolic but sacramental.

—C. S. Lewis, *The Weight of Glory*

The greatest thing a human soul ever does in this world is to see something, and tell what it saw in a plain way. Hundreds of people can talk for one who can think, but thousands can think for one who can see.

—John Ruskin

The legendary music producer Rick Rubin recently wrote a book about artistry entitled *The Creative Act: A Way of Being*. As a punk rock kid, he ran into Russell Simmons and heard something different and compelling in this new genre of hip-hop. He worked with Johnny Cash at a low point for Cash and drew him to new heights with songs like "Hurt." Rubin has worked with a diverse array of great artists: from the Beastie Boys and Run-DMC to Metallica and Slayer to the Avett Brothers. All along, he's been able to draw out the best in artists—not through linear steps but through a way of being (as his title suggests). He has a unique gift of listening and harnessing power inherent in people.

At the beginning of his book, he writes, "To live as an artist is a way of being in the world. A way of perceiving. Refining our sensitivity to tune into the more subtle notes."[1] Though Rubin presides by a more Buddhist-guru ethic, he's on to something deeply human and deeply Christian. It echoes our proposal in this book: to be creative is to be human, and to be a creative human is to function by a way of attention. Whether you call yourself an artist or not, you do create something—whether that be the nurture of children, spreadsheets, a healthier mind, or business proposals. As such, we must be attentive to our way of being. A sacramental imagination can help artists, sure, but it can also help everyone regardless of creative calling. The sacraments help us more rightly attend to the true reality of the world: by beholding, we can be attuned to the beauty behind every material thing.

Here's how Dietrich von Hildebrand describes the effect of beholding beauty:

> [O]ur heart is filled with a desire for loftier regions about which this beauty speaks, and it looks upward with longing. In order to behold this beauty, we need not know God, much less think of him, for, objectively, there is a reflection of God in these things, not merely in the manner with which all that exists portrays God, but by having something *appear* in things of a relatively low ontological rank, which in a special manner announces God in its quality. Only when we have understood this quasi-sacramental function of the visible and audible, this mystery that God has entrusted to it, can we do justice to the function of this beauty in the life of the redeemed . . . (Beauty) contains summons.[2]

It is this "quasi-sacramental summoning" to which we now turn. The material matters because it shows something of the spiritual presence of God. We don't look at the mere material object (materialist) or past the material object (spiritualist) but in and through the object to the divine Creator. Since God makes all things, everything has God's imprint. This is an echo of Psalm 19:2: "The heavens declare the glory of God." The cosmos is full of significance, so "God calls us to see the world as packed with meaning, a living book, a world of metaphor."[3] Our task is not to manufacture or assign meaning but to discover what is already there. God's choice of revelation is through created things.

---

1. Rubin, *Creative Act*, 2.

2. Hildebrand, *Beauty in the Light of Redemption*, 22.

3. Myers, *Poetics of Orthodoxy*, 94.

DEFINING THE SACRAMENTAL

The sacraments—baptism and the Lord's Supper in the Protestant tradition—are defined in the Catechism of the Book of Common Prayer (1662) as "an outward and visible sign of an inward and spiritual grace."[4] The sacraments are physical, material objects (and actions) that point to an invisible, spiritual reality. Hans Boersma, referencing his Christian Platonist leanings, extends the sacraments beyond their meaning in Holy Baptism and the Lord's Supper. According to Boersma, "everything around us is sacramental, in the sense that everything God has created both points to him and makes him present."[5] Baptism and the Eucharist are unique sacraments that are given particular significance, but every created thing has a sacramental quality, to a lesser degree, because it shares in the life of God. This sacramental understanding of the world is to affirm that "God reveals himself through created things . . . that God can speak through the things he created."[6] Key to a sacramental vision is an understanding of this reality: God reveals himself through created things. There is shared holiness in created things, and they shine like transfigurations when used rather than enjoyed. Ordinary things are not to be enjoyed as ultimate but are used en route to the ultimate enjoyment, God. This Augustinian distinction is key to how one interacts with the world of things. Just as one sees through the particular sacraments to the divine grace and reality behind them, so we are invited to see through ordinary objects to the divine. The sacraments teach us something about God. Through baptism and the Lord's Supper, we are not projecting meaning upon the material elements but drawing out the meaning latent within them. Material reality is holy because God speaks through it. The particular sacraments are the unveiling of God's glory hidden in water and bread and wine, and then when eyes turn toward other ordinary objects—a flower, a mountainside, or a bowl of fruit—one has eyes to behold holy transfiguration. The sacraments are pedagogical for a sacramental imagination.

The incarnation provides the basis for how we understand the sacramental imagination. The sacramental joining of human and divine natures in Christ should lead us to recognize the natural and heavenly worlds as

---

4. This section borrows from Alex's article, "Going to School with Marilynne Robinson."

5. Boersma, *Scripture as Real Presence*, 1.

6. Vander Zee, *Christ Baptism and the Lord's Supper*, 17.

intermingling. This connection in Jesus led many of the early church fathers to conclude that because Scripture and creation derive from the same divine source, a consistent mode of communication should be expected in both Scripture and creation. This forms our understanding of nature as part of a system where nature signifies invisible spiritual truths in a variety of ways. The union of the earthly and heavenly within Christ provides us with an analogical and anagogical principle that leads us to consider how all created things demonstrate this earthly and heavenly relationship. In other words, this vision leads us upward.[7]

This sacramental approach provides us with a model for interpreting the Old Testament, moving the interpreter beyond the literal meaning of the words in order to discover the fullest truth. Old Testament "types" (people, events, images, rituals) point us toward a deeper meaning in the New Testament realities in which they participate—this doesn't make the Old Testament less meaningful, instead, every event, character, ritual has even more significance because of it's divine role in revealing and reflecting Christ. This way of interpretation is significant for artists because it reinforces a sacramental principle that directs our eyes through surface images—whether it be the literal meaning of words (Scripture) or a created form (nature)—in order to discover a deeper meaning. This approach to the Old Testament might seem inconsequential to our life as artists; however, we should recognize the way of interpreting Scripture forms habits related to seeing. A spiritual reading of Scripture calls us to interpret the Old Testament as patterned after Christ and pointing toward him. The Book of Nature reveals in a similar manner and is thus filled with meaning because of its Source.

This sacramental interpretation of Scripture led many of the early church fathers to take a poetic approach to the Scriptures. These labels did not come as a result of their artistic capabilities. Instead, they exhibited an artistic imagination. The desire of the church fathers to see Christ in the Old Testament was carried over into the way they looked at creation. They weren't projecting their own meaning *onto* Scripture, but drawing meaning out of Scripture. God's poetic joining in Christ led them to a symbolic reading of the Bible, and further, conditioned their vision of the world. They read the Bible sacramentally, then came to see the world in the same light. While the incarnation of Christ and the sacraments provide a basis for understanding the earthly and spiritual joining, the allegorical reading

7. See de Lubac, *Medieval Exegesis*, 180.

of Scripture, common in the early church, exemplifies how recognizing these corresponding realities trains our eyes to see God throughout all creation. It makes sense that God's way of communicating his divine character would be consistent and should be carried over from Christ to Scripture to the sacraments, and then, from the sacraments to all creation.

A compelling way to think about the sacraments comes from the Eastern rather than the Western church. The term for Eucharist in Syriac is *raza*. The plural of *raza* is *raze*, "mysteries."[8] It's generative to consider that in the Syriac tradition *raza* can be translated as mystery, sacrament, symbol, or secret. As Sebastian Brock reflects on St. Ephrem the Syrian, he says, "Outward historical meaning and inner spiritual meaning of scripture are as intimately intermingled and linked as are body and soul in the human person and humanity and divinity in Christ."[9] The meaning of reality is hidden in the symbol of the bread and wine. Mystery and reality exist together. The way to approach this mystery of sacrament is through contemplation. God is wrapped in mystery. There is no other way to see reality through the mystery without the imagination. And to the imagination we now turn.

DISCERNING THE REAL: THE ROLE OF IMAGINATION

Lawrence Sullivan studied the way myths are used by indigenous peoples in the Amazon River basin. He discovered that myths are not mere lore or fake but "significations that reveal the nature of significance, they make effective metastatements about imaginal existence."[10] Reflecting on this reality as applied to a theological aesthetic, Alejandro García-Rivera notes that this makes the imagination a function of both sense and intellect. He goes on, "The understanding of imagination proposed here is not an epistemology but a theological aesthetics. Imagination is not so much a servant of knowledge as it is an aesthetics of mystery . . . In other words, the imagination is the prime mover and movement of the human heart."[11] García-Rivera defines a theological aesthetic this way: that which moves the human heart. The aesthetic activates the faculty of the imagination. As such, the sacramental vision occurs at the intersection of reason and

8. Brock, *Luminous Eye*, 41.

9. Brock, *Luminous Eye*, 48.

10. Sullivan, *Icanchu's Drum*, 22.

11. García-Rivera, *Community of the Beautiful*, 24–25.

imagination, comprehension and apprehension. These faculties are not in competition but exist in harmony.

The poet Malcolm Guite argues along the same lines. He suggests, "The purpose of imagination, in its playfulness and poetry in particular, is to be a bridge between reason and intuitive apprehension, to find for apprehension just those shapes, those local habitations and names, that make for comprehension. We must not distrust the longings of the imagination."[12] As such, Guite defines the imagination as "a truth-bearing faculty, and more than that it is an appeal to artists, poets, sculptors, storytellers, and filmmakers to kindle our imaginations for Christ, who is himself the kindling imagination of God, who brings all things into being."[13] So while the imagination, or imagining, often corresponds to something that is imaginary, the sacramental imagination relates more to drawing out real meaning than projecting meaning onto a form.

Experiencing the world like this is given to us by God, not something we manufacture. Artists function as creatives by identifying material symbols that correspond with heavenly ideas. Sacramental artists are not burdened to find appropriate symbols to represent ideas. Rather, through a trained imagination, they are tasked to trace out associations that already exist throughout creation. C. S. Lewis puts it this way: "For me, reason is the natural organ of truth; but imagination is the organ of meaning. Imagination, producing new metaphors or revivifying old, is not the cause of truth, but its condition."[14] Jean Daniélou comments that the imagination is the faculty that "*discovers* a real content through symbolic appearance."[15] The mind, then, is not a passive substance but a living power and active agent. This imagining requires glancing, observing, looking, and then creating, transforming, and embodying forth what one sacredly observes. Contemplation is the key that allows us to see.

More pointedly, the novelist and poet (and farmer) Wendell Berry is worth quoting at length on the imagination:

> The term imagination in what I take to be its truest sense refers to a mental faculty that some people have used and throughout about with the utmost seriousness. The sense of the verb "to imagine" contains the full richness of the verb "to see." To imagine is to see

<hr>

12. Guite, *Faith, Hope and Poetry*, 58.

13. Guite, *Lifting the Veil*, 11.

14. Lewis, "Bluspels and Flalansferes," 265.

15. Daniélou, *Lord of History*, 135.

most clearly, familiarly, and understandingly with the eyes, but also to see inwardly, with the "mind's eye." It is to see, not passively, but with a force of vision and even with visionary force. To take it seriously we must give up at once any notion that imagination is disconnected from reality or truth or knowledge . . . I will say, from my own belief and experience, that the imagination thrives on contact, on tangible connections.[16]

The imagination teaches us how to see. The training to see is based on tangible connections rather than artificial projections. The imagination is not merely for children or artists; it is for every living human. We all imagine the world a certain way, and Jesus helps reframe how we imagine the world—this world and the world to come. Our task is to faithfully live into that vision of divine reality, which is sometimes veiled. Modernity may mask the presence of God in symbols, but with a sacramental imagination, we reveal what has always been present within creation, namely the marks of God's handiwork.

Samuel Taylor Coleridge once wrote, "The noblest gift of Imagination is the power of discerning the cause in the effect a power which when employed on the works of the Creator elevates and by the variety of it's pleasures almost monopolizes the Soul. We see our God everywhere—the Universe in the most literal sense is his written language."[17] It was this mystical edge that the Romantics held in common, especially in confrontation with the rationalism of their day. In modernity, "we have lost our sense of the sanctified imagination that can show us a world of deep meaning and permanent truth."[18] George McDonald applauded Wordsworth for the role he played in opposing the intellectualism that seeped into modern theology, stating, "The divine expressions of Nature, that is, the face of the Father therein visible, began to heal the plague which the worship of knowledge had bred."[19]

The problem with many of the Romantic poets, including much of Wordsworth's early writings, was that their writings verged on pantheism.[20]

16. Berry, *It All Turns on Affection*, 14.

17. Quoted in Fraser, *Beauty and Belief*, 34.

18. Quoted in Myers, *Poetics of Orthodoxy*, 92.

19. Prickett, *Romanticism and Religion*, 71.

20. The priest-chef Robert Farrar Capon provides a helpful corrective. His exalted view of material things should not be mistaken for idolatry. He writes, "Things must be met for themselves. To take them only for their meaning is to convert them into gods—to make them too important, and therefore to make *them* unimportant altogether. Idolatry

Wordsworth believed nature to have inherent values to convey, and the capacity to inspire imagination regardless of the state of the viewer. However, we are arguing that the sacramental effect necessitates a translucent viewer. Just as the sacraments do not take effect without a faithful believer receiving them, so a sacramental imagination is not effective without faithful eyes.

Coleridge depended on Augustine's doctrine of illumination. In essence, the illumination did not occur within reason or with some inner light of the imagination. Rather, following Augustine, illumination was from the outside, a light shining on the imagination. Commenting on this development, Malcolm Guite writes, "We do not, in fact, come to a perception of the world, or any understanding of it, as a result of a series of logical deductions of calculations of the discursive reason. It is not the case that a certain quantum of manipulable data falls, as it were, ready-made into the mind through senses, and then we make the necessary calculations to make sense of it, but rather that our minds and hearts go out to embrace the world imaginatively."[21] The world shines, and we are invited into seeing the glimmers of the world with our imagination—something in between mind and affection. The effectiveness of the sign depends on our cultivation of the lenses through which we view the world.

In essence, imagination is the faculty that asks, "What do you see?" before the brain kicks on. This line of thought is reminiscent of the Anglican Tractarian John Keble. In his tract on mysticism, he is worth quoting at length:

> The question is like that of the general evidences of religion: a person who would go into it with advantage, should he imbued beforehand with a kind of natural piety, which will cause him to remember all along, that perhaps, when he comes to the end of this inquiry, he will find that God was all the while really there. He will "put off his shoes from off his feet," if he do but think it possible that an angel may tell him, by and by, "The place where thou standest is holy ground." So it must be, in some measure, with every right-minded person, in the examination of every practice and opinion, against which the charge of Mysticism is brought. Whatever may appear in the case at first sight, likely to move scorn or ridicule, or tempt to mere lightness of thought; it will be an exercise of faith, a trial of a serious heart, to repress for the time any

---

has two faults. It is not only a slur on the true God; it also an insult to true things." Capon, *Supper of the Lamb*, 20.

21. Guite, *Faith, Hope and Poetry*, 172.

tendency of that kind: the loss and error being infinitely greater, if we are found trifling with a really sacred subject, than if we merely prove to have been a little more serious than was necessary. In this sense, that is to say in regard of the reverent or irreverent *temper*, in which such inquiries may be approached, superstition is surely a great deal better than irreligion: whatever may be thought of the abstract question, Whether it be the safer extreme to believe too much, or too little?[22]

The key to seeing the world in such a light is love. Love and wonder pulls us up toward God in theological reflection. Our disposition, our imagination, our habit of being needs a redirection to care to see.

REIMAGINING THE WORLD

Before describing how a sacramental imagination can and should affect artists, it will be helpful to consider the errors that may come from a disordered or misdirected vision. We are often tempted to take on a diminished vision of the world by choosing a material or a spiritual lens, which causes us to undervalue the role of beauty in our artistic creations.

An overly spiritualist imagination is one that assumes a world that is emptied of transcendent meaning. Such a vision can project our present circumstances as having no significance. It is often the case that Christians, like the gnostics, believe that material obscures the truth about God because the divine could not be present in a broken world. So, the result of this way of being would naturally lead us to disregard our earthly experience and result in a disembodied faith where God is detached from creation, and our faith is only useful for a future heavenly existence.

The materialist imagination does not look past the world, but looks squarely upon it. While the spiritualist claim is that there is nothing to see here, the materialist believes that this is all there is to see. It is a disenchanted way of understanding that focuses attention on the form, while neglecting to recognize a meaning beyond things as they appear. The following charts are an attempt to demonstrate the way a divided vision plays out in real circumstances. A sacramental imagination is given by God and is formed in worship *and* forms our worship. Our approach to the sacraments and interpretation, both, reflect our imagination, and have a vital role in shaping it.

22. Keble, "On the Mysticism," 3.

FIGURE 1

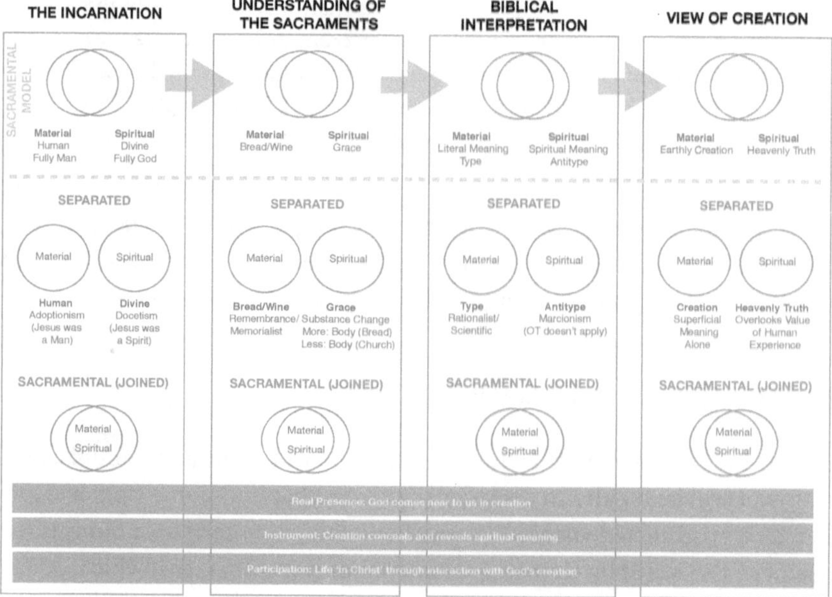

A materialist approach to the sacraments may trend toward a memorialist view of Holy Communion that emphasizes remembering as the primary motivation for observing the Eucharist. For instance, the bread and the wine are necessary, but they are not usually recognized as delivering unseen grace. While remembering is an essential element of Holy Communion for the memorialist, it's possible that meaning is found in the act itself, which places the focus on recipients, rather than what is being given by God. Sentiments from this view might sound like: "If you observe Communion every week, it will lose its meaning." This suggests that meaning is what we make of it, rather than finding meaning that is not dependent on or gauged by emotion.

On the other hand, a spiritualist view of the Eucharist might direct attention away from the bread and wine—perhaps it becomes something else—which could downplay the necessity of the literal elements. This view might be prone to superstition, with little regard for the importance of the gathering, or on remembering. These are two examples of the possible influences of a divided materialist and spiritualist approach to the Eucharist. In the table below, we've provided some ideas about the potential effect of an isolated view, and how a sacramental imagination joins the two. Figure

2 applies the sacramental model to a variety of areas, inviting us to consider the way having either a materialist or spiritualist vision influences our understanding of the faith, and further affects our everyday work. How might a materialist or spiritualist vision be revealed in our particular vocation and what are the potential outcomes of this divided way of seeing? Does having an either-or approach lead us to believe and practice in ways that lack the depth that comes from a sacramental vision? In the next chapter, we will explore how seeing leads us toward a more creative, and thus, fulfilling vocation.

CONTEXT	"LOOK AT" (MATERIALIST)	"LOOK PAST" (SPIRITUALIST)	"LOOK INTO" (THROUGH) (SACRAMENTALIST)
Material / Spiritual diagrams	Material	Spiritual	Material / Spiritual
Religion	• Know This… • Bible Studies • Social Justice	• Pray This… • Prayer Meetings • Escape Creation/World	• Ritual Participation (Embodied Prayers) • Knowledge Finds its Fullness in Experience • God is Present to Us In/Through Creation
Christian Life/Salvation	• Doing Good or Knowing More • Works: Save the World/Lives	• Getting "Saved" (Disembodied) • Works: Save Souls	• Being Saved Through Our Bodies • Works: Participation in Christ
Worship	• Improve Your Life (Practical) • *Do* More or *Know* More	• A Transcendent Experience • *Feel* Saved • Looking Beyond Worries of Life (No Time to Lament)	• Sacramental Participation: Praying Scripture, Praying with our Bodies, Participation in the Eucharist Joins Heavenly and Earthly Realities
Art	• Overt Representation • Imitation • Formalism • Sentimentalism (Commiseration)	• Overt Representation • Fancy (Unrealistic) • Suprematism • Sentimentalism (Idealism)	• Subtle: Room for Mystery to Exist • Symbolic/Analogical Representation • Imminent/Transcendent Qualities • Draws Us Into Contemplation

Pastoral Reflections:
Seeing the World Sacramentally

THE SACRED/SECULAR DIVIDE IS not a problem just for artists. All who live in the modern age are affected by the materialist/spiritualist divide. Likewise, all vocations feel the plague of the modern divide. The agrarian writer Wendell Berry comments on modernism's dualism: "It is a cleavage, a radical discontinuity, between Creator and creature, spirit and matter, religion and nature, religion and economy, worship and work, etc. This dualism, I think, is the most destructive disease that afflicts us. In its best known, its most dangerous, and perhaps its fundamental version, it is the dualism of body and soul."[1]

So while this book is aimed at artists, a sacramental imagination is not only for artistic imagination. A sacramental imagination is a way of being in the world that helps us see divine presence in created things. It is a holistic vision that unites whole and holy being in the world. Wendell Berry has been insistent about this divide in agriculture. In his legendary *The Unsettling of America: Culture and Agriculture*, Berry paints a path forward. He writes, "The concept of health is rooted in the concept of wholeness. To be healthy is to be whole."[2] Likewise, we want to suggest that central to a sacramental imagination is a healthy wholeness, a bringing together of spirit and matter, body and soul, reason and imagination.

The modern division afflicts the way we view the world, particularly in our vocation. We want to paint a picture of sacramental vocation to help all readers reorientate to the world.

1. Berry, "Christianity and the Survival of Creation."
2. Berry, *Unsettling of America*, 103.

FIGURE 3

SACRAMENTAL VOCATION

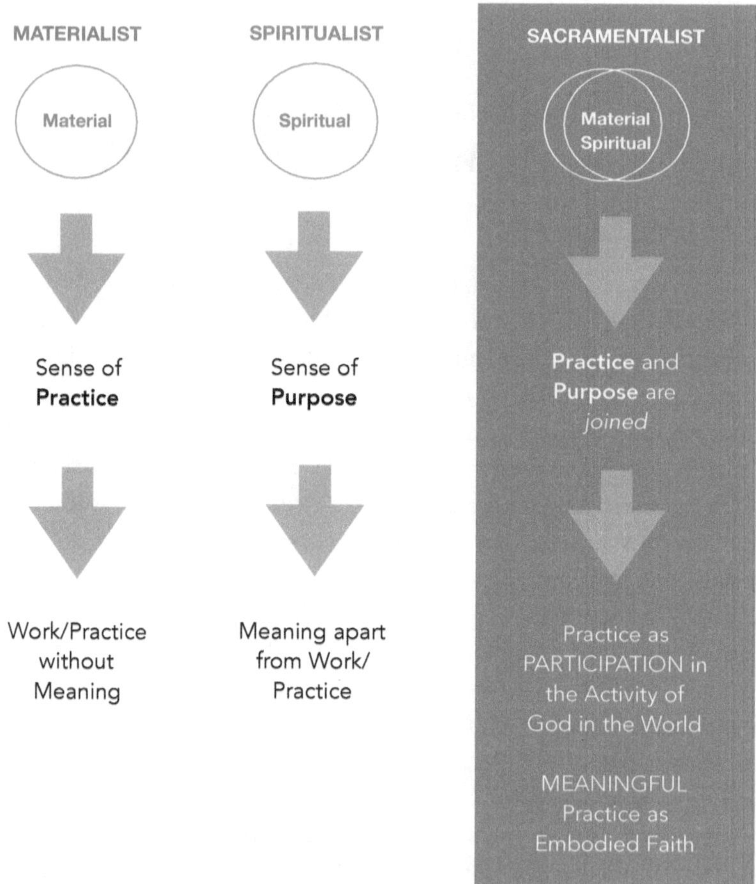

On the one hand, a material view of creation views vocation pragmatically. Torn from meaning, your job is a means to pay the bills but there isn't much purpose or belonging in it. It's utilitarian, and this divide, as Berry posits, causes the abuse of people, land, and the world. So while this view of vocation is material, it leads to the destruction of God's material world, viewing labor as a means to an end, thus using resources in exploitation. This divided view empties the earthly substance of spiritual meaning, which can lead to a disembodied faith that regards God as impersonal and experienced only from a distance.

On the other hand, spiritualism reduces vocation to religious purpose. Either your vocation is an interruption from the more meaningful work of church work or devotions, or it's turned to an avenue for evangelism. There is purpose and meaning involved, yet the main thrust of life is the "religious" or "ecclesial" stuff.

For instance, let's take the vocation of a mother. In one sense, a mother can be seen as a utilitarian caregiver. Sometimes mothers don't derive much meaning but, being beckoned and called constantly by young children, their existence can seem to be reduced to a food provider that keeps the children alive. Many mothers feel this lack of meaning and purpose in raising young children as it's easy to feel like they aren't doing anything "significant."

Or, for a more spiritualist view, the main meaning can be found in leading personal devotions, discipline, and spiritual or intellectual growth. Feeding the kids, driving them around, organizing playdates are merely necessary burdens that make the really "good stuff" happen.

Berry suggests another way forward:

> If, on the other hand, we believe that we are living souls, God's dust and God's breath, acting our parts among other creatures all made of the same dust and breath as ourselves; and if we understand that we are free, within the obvious limits of mortal human life, to do evil or good to ourselves and to the other creatures—then all our acts have a supreme significance. If it is true that we are living souls and morally free, then all of us are artists. All of us makers, within mortal terms and limits, of our lives, of one another's lives, of things we need and use.[3]

Applying this to the role of mothering, all a mother's acts have supreme significance—from breastfeeding and changing diapers to taking the kids to church and singing them songs. We are all makers, in the words of Berry, operating in the material and spiritual realm, because that's who we are: God's dust and God's breath. We nurture both in our lives.

In many ways, this accords to Frederick Buechner's popular definition of vocation: the "place where your great passion meets the world's great need."[4] The world's great need is important—people need shelter for their bodies, financial advice for their bank accounts, healing for their bodies,

---

3. Berry, "Christianity and the Survival of Creation."
4. Buechner, *Wishful Thinking*, 95.

etc. The physical really and truly matters. Likewise, you have a great passion—a passion to make a home, to feel loved, to provide support, to make a difference. A sacramental vocation exists at those intersections—where both the material and spiritual are seen, noticed, cultivated, and loved. From street sweeping to preaching, all of us work in the dust-breath that God calls souls. We are called to cultivate the material that God entrusts to us in a holistic and healing manner. We are all makers and artists.

To show how a sacramental vocation may affect one's vision of work, here is our friend Kevin Ude describing his creative vision through game making:

> "Do you understand the rules to this game?"
>
> "I think we'll figure it out, if we just start playing.
>
> I'm a board game designer. It's a creative endeavor that blends aesthetic sensibilities, mathematical thinking, and human unpredictability. But what is my art form's medium? The supplies I have are card stock and cardboard, wood, and plastic bits. The effort and energy I spend go into working out the rules and the game mechanics, finding the right balance of challenge that is neither so easy that it is uninteresting nor so hard that it is frustrating. The thing I'm actually trying to craft, however, is the experience the players will have, something ephemeral.
>
> Is the game the cards and dice, the physical components? Is the game the rules? Is the game the experience that happens to the players as they play? As I learn more about living this life sacramentally, developing my sacramental imagination, my craft of game design and my spiritual understanding seem to be continually informing one another. Is Communion the bread and wine, the physical elements? Is Communion the liturgy, the rules we follow? Is Communion the experience that happens inside the communicant? And is there a way to get better answers without even asking the right questions?
>
> A significant part of what makes board games so appealing to so many is that all of these things matter, and all of them are present. The physical does matter. The clack of dominoes, mahjong tiles, and poker chips is a lot of the attraction of those games. Staid and solemn adults become downright playful when loud plastic is within reach. Mathematically, a game would work just the same if in place of rolling dice, you used a computer-generated list of random numbers. Or suppose, before coming for game night, your friend

sat down and rolled some dice over and over, writing down all of the results in a list. Then, any time you needed a die roll in a game, they just read you the next number from the list. How frustrating. How dead. Physical things matter. In the moment. The texture, the weight, the sound, and the feel matter. Experiencing the world sacramentally is experiencing with our senses, not just our intellect.

It's common among board game designers to dread writing out the rules to a game they're working on. It's also common to describe it as invaluable. You have to determine what the players need to know, and in what order. You also must determine what to not say, what would just add unnecessary complexity, or what is just strategy advice that the players would do better to discover for themselves. In this day and age, outside the world of games (or sacraments), we tend to think we can do everything best in words, just explain it all. But I'm learning that part of what I love about sacraments and sacramentality, in general, is that mere words can't do some things. I'm one of those people who enjoys reading the rules to new games. I'm always happy to be the one to read the rules and teach everyone else. But I know that I never really know how to play a game until I sit down with friends or family and actually play the game.

"Do you understand the rules to this game?"

"I think we'll figure it out, if we just start playing."

That's the right way to do it. It sometimes means you have to refer back to the rule book, but it's also the only reason you knew you didn't understand fully and needed clarification.

So it is with sacramental living. The standard is to not understand things fully, but after a hand or two you catch on to the basics, and some things only make sense once you actually start playing. Not only that, but the more games you play the more you'll get. Some art only exists for a single interaction, you see it once or read it once, and then move on to the next thing. With a few exceptions, board games are meant to be returned to again and again. They are specifically created so that you can have a new and unique experience every time you play. In some ways, they exist to create a space where things can happen.

There is also a depth beyond the surface participation. It's not just levers to pull to make the machine work. Deep participation is necessary to discover some unknown realities, to uncover hidden things. Many people play chess, or *Settlers of Catan*, or *Magic: The Gathering* thousands upon thousands of times, for years and years.

They keep discovering new interactions, surprising each other with unexpected plays, delighting over the challenge of responding to their opponent's insight, the tumble of the dice, the shuffle of the deck. One of the great joys of being a game designer is knowing that every time one of my creations is played, the players are also creating. They take the "game" I made, but they make a new and unique game of it by the way they interact, the way they respond to the randomizers, the way they work the rules to their own advantage. Edith Schaeffer, in her book *Hidden Art*, first drew my attention to the fact that we are created in the image of a Creator, so we get to participate in creation. The sacramental way is participation. We're called to sing a new song, but when we play a game we can't help but play a new game.

4

Creative Ways of Being and Seeing: The Artistic Sacramental Imagination

To live as an artist is a way of being in the world. A way of perceiving. A practice of paying attention. Refining our sensitivity to tune in to the more subtle notes. Looking for what draws us in and what pushes us away. Noticing what feeling tones arise and where they lead.

—RICK RUBIN

To produce in beauty the artist must be in love with beauty.

—JACQUES MARITAIN

LIKELY, IF YOU'VE HEARD of a Christian visual artist, the name you know is Makoto Fujimura. Fujimura is a Japanese-American who specializes in abstract expressionism. As one of us regularly describes him, he's not a famous Christian artist, but he's a renowned artist who happens to be a Christian. His work is known not just in the Christian world, but in cultural centers. His expositions have been featured in the top art galleries in the world and even as he displays his Christian convictions, secular audiences still appreciate his work.

As an expressionist artist, one could label him as a postmodern or a sentimental spiritualist. There is no material object that he typically represents. However, in hearing about Mako's work, it isn't merely the feeling or idea that matters to him. Both the material and sentiment play into his work. While his paintings may not display any material thing, he cares deeply about the material with which he creates. He uses the material world to communicate something, even if the image isn't concrete. In describing his collaboration with Ellen Davis to paint all 150 Psalms, Fujimura explains his slow art by his choice of material elements: "sumi ink (sticks made from pine shoots that I must rub against a stone for more than an hour) and oyster shell whites (pulverized oyster shells that require more than three years to create and then take me a day and a half to reconstitute). I am also using platinum and gold powders . . ."[1] These material components mean something; by their use, they communicate not just the artistic process but the artistic product. Fujimura values the preciousness of materials, stones, and minerals as he creates his abstract work. As such, we want to suggest that he is one example of the way a sacramental imagination influences artistic expression. His vision has been cultivated in his creative work. Rather than use art as in materialism or explain art as in spiritualism, art has a sacramental character in that it invites viewers into contemplation and enjoyment. The form and the idea matter together but art cannot be reduced to either form or idea. There's a mystery of beyondness to this way of creating that shifts our impression in subtle and gradual ways. Jennifer Allen Craft, who will share later in this book, claims, "As we lift up signs in our eucharistic participation or in the wider sign-making practices of the arts, we acknowledge the spiritual dimension of physical materials—the ways in which we can experience God's presence in bread and wine, or even paint and wax—as active encounters with God through the material world."[2] In Fujimura's materials, he encounters God through his slow art, and he invites the viewer to encounter God through his material creation.

But in a world where God's presence has been washed away, where his weight and influence seem no longer present or at least considered a factor in the world, how may artists like Fujimura help viewers reimagine reality? Better, how can we connect with and embody such an imagination? George Steiner suggests a way forward: "We must look on the world *as if* created and respond to it *as if* to the 'real presence of the transcendental' and especially in an era of secularization, the artist must 'make a wager on transcendence.'"[3] The secular world still uses the language of movement, touch, and power with art. Viewers flock to galleries and studios searching

---

1. Fujimura, *Art+Faith*, 38.
2. Craft, *Placemaking and the Arts*, 205.
3. Steiner, *Real Presences*, 229–30, cited in Howes, *Art of the Sacred*, 154.

for transcendence—even if that's not what they would name it. As artists with a sacramental imagination, we must make a wager on transcendence.

DEFENDING THE SACRAMENTAL PRINCIPLE

There are some necessary clarifications in using the term "sacrament" in light of recent scholarship in theology and the arts. By interacting with Junius Johnson and Jeremy Begbie, we want to defend the use of the term "sacramental" in referring to the arts. Johnson offers a companion to our understanding, while Begbie questions the use of such a term in the work of theologians like David Brown.

Johnson wrote a theology of beauty titled *The Father of Lights*. He discusses the terms of sacrament and icon, and how each provides avenues to the divine. For us, the issue is a little semantic, but we bring it to the reader's attention to make a few important distinctions.

For Johnson, both sacraments and icons provide access to the divine in distinct ways.[4] Both icons and sacraments are creaturely signs. A sacrament is a particular way of imagining God by his imbuing creation with the divine presence in a traditional way. In other words, bread has a direct correlation to a body, wine has a direct correlation to blood, and water has a direct correlation to cleansing. There's a straightforward relationship in sacraments between sign and symbol as opposed to iconography, which requires a bit more insider understanding of pictures, symbols, colors, etc. Further, rather than bringing the divine reality to us, icons transfer us into divine presence through traditional forms. Icons are a bridge that the mind walks but do not become what they signify.

These are important distinctions, yet we prefer the term "sacramentality" when it comes to art and artists. Perhaps we could describe artists as sacramental iconographers. We, as image bearers, are icons of God, and so we act as icons in creation. With a sacramental imagination, artists are sign makers. We see the world imbued with meaning and take on the symbolism of the creation in our creations. Out of this vision, artists might see themselves as iconographers in the sense that we prayerfully work to bring others to encounter God. As in good art, we desire to lead the viewer upward rather than merely outward. However, our art does not function as "windows to heaven" as typical iconography does. Our art is not a portal out of this world but a way of seeing this world with sacramental vision. We

---

4. See specifically Johnson, *Father of Lights*, 172–73.

invite the visual realities to become present to us in new ways rather than transporting us somewhere else. This requires, like icons, holy contemplation and attention. We invite contemplation of divine reality by participating with God in the world of created things. We use "sacramental" in a vision of the world rather than what the art is.

Second, we want to address some concerns raised by the theologian Jeremy Begbie.[5] It may be a semantic issue for Begbie. Perhaps he prefers incarnational over sacramental, and the issue would be cleared up. However, we think the sacramental is worth explaining. There has been a rise in the term "sacramental" or "sacramentality" in regard to theology and the arts. Begbie's main contention, drawing on Rowan Williams, is a question that must be answered: "How does presence *alter* things?"[6] That is, if the sacramental principle includes the presence of the divine, how does that presence alter things in art? Junius Johnson argues that the sacraments make present culture. In other words, the sacramental character of art makes an artist's cultural background or cultural complexities present. We can accept that, though this movement takes place on a horizontal level rather than vertical, as you remember, the plane of great art. Good art can draw something out of us or reveal something, but great art pulls us upward, leads to a sense of deeper dignity, and reveals the divine.

As we use the term "sacramental," we are not merely referring to the product which the artist creates. When we say sacramental, we are referring more to the artist's vision than what their art is. The divine presence, in this sense, changes an artist's way of seeing. When we participate with God in the act of seeing and therefore creating, it leads us into contemplation of the divine, and therefore the divine realities become present to us. It may reveal an invisible reality through a visible thing, and when our vision is in harmony with the divine, Christ is made present. By using the term "sacramental" we are saying artists produce something with sacramental vision rather than designating the produced artwork as sacramental. The vision is what we're after, which is why we can offer no "three steps to sacramental artwork." It requires a vision, a posture, or as Flannery O'Connor calls it, "a habit of being."

5. Begbie, *Peculiar Orthodoxy*, 190.
6. Williams, "Presence," 4.

THE HABIT OF ART

We are big fans of Flannery O'Connor. O'Connor was influenced by Jacques Maritain's artistic philosophy, and she developed Maritain's concept of "the habit of art." Art is not merely a discipline one takes up but a way of looking at the world that involves one's whole personality. O'Connor describes the concept as "a way of looking at the created world and of using the senses so as to make them find as much meaning as possible in things."[7]

In an introduction to O'Connor's letters, Sally Fitzgerald explains the connections between Maritain and O'Connor.[8] She defines a habit of being as "an excellence not only of action but of interior disposition and activity that increasingly reflected the object, the being, which specified it, and was itself reflected in what she did and said."[9] The cultivation of a disposition is what we're after in this book. We will use a lot of words, but we know these words will be insufficient if it only affects your head and does not affect your eyes. Your eyes are the source of your vision and imagination. And vision takes time and habits to adjust.

We love the way O'Connor describes the connection between beliefs and vision. She argues that, for the fiction writer, "Your beliefs will be the light by which you see, but they will not be what you see and they will not be a substitute for seeing." In other words, while your beliefs may be there, your beliefs are fundamentally aesthetic—they involve the eye. As such, she goes on, "this is something that can't be learned only in the head; it has to be learned in the habits. It has to become a way that you habitually look at things."[10] Vision is shaped through habits of being. It takes the imagination.

In this way, artists sometimes have an advantage over theologians in sacramental sensing, or at least as theologians are trained in the modern age. As pastors and theologians, we're equipped to say things. We talk about abstract issues, theological problems, and ethereal people. However, good artists (and good theologians) show things rather than merely say things. Showing things requires concrete examples, specific people, and real situations. These developments take time. It takes time to develop the habit of seeing the world, and showing people the way, rather than telling them what to believe. Beliefs are present, but they are within the context of vision. You

---

7. O'Connor, *Mystery and Manners*, 101.

8. We borrow this section from Alex's article "Ahhh I See."

9. Fitzgerald, Introduction to O'Connor, *Habit of Being*, xvii.

10. O'Connor, *Mystery and Manners*, 91–92.

can tell someone what to believe, but if their vision is disordered, the beliefs will exist in incongruence with their vision. Artists are those who show. Showing necessitates a theological vision, a habit of being, an incarnational imagination.

O'Connor challenges artists with this incarnational and thus sacramental vision. She writes, "Fiction is about everything human and we are made out of dust, and if you scorn getting yourself dusty, then you shouldn't try to write fiction. It's not a grand enough job for you."[11] She does not separate the dustiness of life from the grandeur of fiction; rather, it is through the mundane that the divine is experienced. We want to challenge visual artists the same way: if you scorn getting dusty, then you shouldn't practice visual arts. The dust enables a sacramental vision, the ability to pay attention and see. Peter Candler Jr. explains O'Connor's anagogical vision this way:

> Thus no independent thing is capable of its own determination as a thing; rather to understand fiction as an incarnational art is to recognize that all things are meaningful only insofar as they all are by virtue of their participation in the divine life and as an expression of the divine glory. Such is the sacramental "reason in making" which constitutes the anagogical imagination, which reveals every visible as a register of the invisible. It is therefore not only as an eschatological reality that creation will be made whole in Christ, it is the beginning of true vision to see the creation groaning now towards its consummation.[12]

Candler insists on "true vision" which can be experienced now, even as we see in a mirror dimly (1 Cor 13:12).

With a sacramental vision, one's art is an exercise of vision, and one's vision is displayed through artistic creation. Therefore, the church's greatest contribution to an artist's life may be the formation of their spiritual vision. Technical training, or even providing artists with opportunities for participation (in an artistic sense), is often the church's main focus when engaging artists. But as churches encourage, training and participation are downstream from vision. We need churches that cultivate vision. The way we perceive the world influences the sort of art we make. The church's central function in the shaping of our artists is to form their imagination, the primary lens through which we perceive the presence of God in the world.

11. O'Connor, *Mystery and Manners*, 68.

12. Candler Jr. "Anagogical Vision of Flannery O'Connor," 19.

Various reasons exist for the malformation of sight, which can result in artists' taking an either/or, materialist or spiritualist approach in their work. A disjoined artistic expression stems from a particular way of observing the world. An isolated material or spiritual vision is consequently revealed in the artist's work. The church provides the space for God to form, or even repair, our divided vision. Charles Taylor suggests that we all respond to transcendent reality, but often misrecognize it.[13] As we gather for worship, our sight is being formed and reformed, our vision is brought into harmony with God in order to appropriately recognize the divine presence in the world. Calibrating our vision with God's is the essential foundation from which art is made, enabling us to pattern our creative activity after Christ's and effectively speak holistic truth into a divided world.

While our lived experience of earthly forms is meaningful, the church's role is to help us see things as they *really* are, to consider the deeper, unseen mysteries as more real than the earthly sign from which they emerge. Sanctification is essential for the development of a sacramental imagination—we are able to live as God has intended as we grow to see things as they truly are. The longing to see God is key to growing in holiness. Hans Boersma states, "We are true to the way God has made us when we make the vision of God our ultimate desire."[14] Likewise, Andrew Louth argues, "If we are to perceive the beauty of God, we need eyes to see it—we need eyes to see it—we need to be transformed by it, purified, illuminated, and finally brought to transfiguring union."[15] This statement indicates a reciprocal relationship between vision and formation. Sacramental vision grows out of holiness, which is necessary for gaining understanding, and at the same time, as we discover these essential truths we grow in holiness. Simply put: the work of perceiving God, the act of searching for where he might be revealed, is both the result of sanctification and is a sanctifying act in itself.

C. S. Lewis connects all these ideas together in a coherent and beautiful way in *The Great Divorce*. He places sight before any other priority of the artist. Lewis describes an encounter between the Spirit and a ghost who had been a famous artist. The ghost is anxious to paint, to stop wasting time and get on with making art. However, the Spirit reminds him that "looking comes first." Having devolved since his earthly experience, the ghost is under the impression that he has seen everything there is to see, which

13. Taylor, *Secular Age*, 768.

14. Boersma, *Seeing God*, 11.

15. Louth, "Beauty Will Save the World," 69.

consequently reduces his work to imitation. Therefore, the Spirit reminds him that his painting on earth was not motivated by a desire to imitate surface realities, but by seeing "glimpses of heaven in the earthly landscapes." The Spirit continues to explain that meaningful art is that which leads others to see beyond things as they appear. Referring to the ghost's way of imitation, the Spirit adds in an almost sarcastic manner, "There is no good telling us about this country, for we see it already." Lewis's Spirit character suggests that in time, and with growth, artists will see better than anyone else, which creates a longing for others to experience the same hidden realities. Despite being eager to begin painting, the ghost is urged to slow down: "at present your business is to see. Come and see."[16]

Artists are naturally anxious to create. While composition and technique are often the focus of growth, Lewis reminds us that creating meaningful art depends first on sight. Sight is an aspect of artistic development that is necessary but is often displaced by our desire to get on with the work of creating. A sacramental vision allows us to see the world rightly by discerning the meaning that is present in and through the layers of superficial realities. The success of a painting is then determined by our desire and ability to identify the glimpses of heaven that are discovered in our vision of earthly landscapes, and then to tell a story about more than is already seen.

A sacramental approach to seeing the world should not cause us to overlook the literal or concrete forms of life. Instead, artists see that God chooses literal forms as vehicles of his grace. Therefore, we should not consider the world as empty of meaning. With a sacramental imagination, we see the world as packed with truths that reveal something of the presence of God.

LOOK AND SEE

The capacity to see God should be sought after and be ever-expanding. For the artist, our ability to see is the basis for interpretation, and thus, our artistic representation. A sacramental imagination enlivens our earthly experience, charging it with meaning and forging a poetic interaction with God in the world. A spiritual imagination, or vision, is something that is formed in us. In the writings that are attributed to Dionysius the Areopagite (referenced in Acts 17:34), the sight of God is placed as a primary pursuit of Christian life, stating, "In most holy contemplation we shall be

16. Lewis, *Great Divorce*, 83–84.

ever filled with the sight of God shining gloriously around us as once it shone for the disciples at the divine transfiguration."[17] He considers the sight of God to be the ultimate aim of humanity. In *The Divine Names*, he proclaims that God is incomprehensible, and to an extent, God remains inaccessible. However, God *does* reveal himself "to each mind in proportion to its capacities."[18] John Henry Newman speaks of a God-given perception that leads us toward a more significant earthly experience as we discover a deeper meaning. In *Apologia Pro Vita Sua*, Newman states,

> Again I ask what would be the thought of a man who when examining a flower, or a herb, or a pebble, or a ray of light, which he treats as something so beneath him in the scale of existence, suddenly discovered that he was in the presence of some powerful being who was hidden behind the visible things he was inspecting,—who, though concealing his wise hand, was giving them their beauty, grace and perfection, as being God's instruments for the purpose,—nay, whose robe and ornaments those objects were, which he was so eager to analyze?[19]

Most artists can relate to seeing all nature as a potential composition—a painting, story, or poem. We are captured by a shape or color. It may be the case that artists have a way of seeing the world that provides them with a unique opportunity to help others see anew. The constant search for the divine presence in the world has a formative effect on our vision. If we are looking for God throughout his creation, we will likely find glimpses of his presence. The activity of looking builds anticipation within us for where God may be found, which leads us to experience the nearness of God, a companionship that comes from sharing in his life through the work of his hand.

A sacramental imagination is God-given, and primarily formed in worship through our participation with God in embodied ways, specifically, in the mysterious interaction with transcendence through the material forms of bread, wine, and water. Worship can form a joined, sacramental vision. For instance, when we partake of the outward and visible forms of the sacraments (bread, wine, and water), we begin to see and experience the way created material is used by God as a vehicle of grace. As we participate in this reality, we come to recognize the various ways that God

17. Dionysius, "Divine Names," 52.

18. Dionysius, "Divine Names," 49.

19. Newman, *Apologia Pro Vita Sua*, 28.

uses natural forms as the means of delivering spiritual nourishment. In *Signs of Grace*, David Brown refers to the role of the sacraments in forming our imagination, stating, "The symbolic aspects of religion show the divine reaching towards us. The symbol is understood as having a divinely given transformative dimension: God as the creator has put something of himself into it, and so it can both engage our imagination and work for our transformation."[20] Brown refers to the way God appeals to the human imagination in a symbolic manner, suggesting that this is how we have been made to learn. We experience union with God through participation. By recognizing the essential role of the material (bread, wine, water) in the sacrament to deliver unseen grace, we are conditioned to expect a similar joining in all creation. Singing in unison, taking postures in prayer, all bring us into tune with God and creation. In particular, the Psalms bring us into sync with Christ as we take on our lips words that Jesus prayed himself.

The symbolic reference between material and spiritual indicates that our spiritual formation depends on more than intellectual learning. God makes use of symbols to appeal to a variety of our senses, which are necessary means of forming our imagination in ways that explanations cannot. Flannery O'Connor states, "The beginning of human knowledge is through the senses, and the fiction writer begins where human perception begins. He appeals through the senses, and you cannot appeal to the senses with abstractions."[21] This manner of communication is reminiscent of the way Christ uses story—he employs real matter as a mediator of infinite ideas, not just as an example (using one thing to explain another), but by displaying the way one participates in the other. O'Connor acknowledges the way Jesus communicates transcendent truths in indirect ways, which is oddly reminiscent of her own practice. Her statement refers to the importance of developing a spiritual imagination for artistic expression, and specifically, the way it will begin to permeate the work of an artist.

In his storytelling, Jesus demonstrates how words can engage our imagination by appealing to various senses. Throughout the Gospels, Jesus' way of telling stories displays the sacramental correspondence between earthly and spiritual realities. When explanations were insufficient for describing the mysteries of God, Jesus referred to created forms as indirect ways of teaching, which served to reveal and conceal aspects of the kingdom of God. Christ used nature in a poetic way to make profound spiritual

20. Brown and Fuller, *Signs of Grace*, ix.
21. O'Connor, *Mystery and Manners*, 67.

truths more accessible to the hearer, and on certain occasions, to veil them from those who were unprepared to receive them.

This poetic manner of speaking reinforced a sacramental model for artistic expression by depicting literal figures as having layers of meaning. In his stories, Jesus displayed the symbolic ways that nature communicates simply by carrying out its intended function. Again, Jesus didn't use these images merely as examples: he was portraying creation as imbued with divine meaning. For example, take Christ as the true vine. Jesus' claim is that he is more vine than a vine is itself. As Luke Bell describes it in *The Meaning of Blue*, "The vine is the expression on its own (less real) level of the divine reality that Jesus Himself is." So, as the argument goes, Jesus is not picking clever word pictures and saying he is those objects, but that there is meaning inherently in objects that the teacher reveals himself in. Bell goes on, "In one sense, the Incarnation is a response to the forgetting of what nature means; it is a direct showing of that meaning."[22]

Christ forms his hearer's hearts through the imagination, and further, shapes their imagination to see the world in a new light. St. Paul acknowledges this way of revealing, stating, "For his invisible attributes, namely, his eternal power and divine nature, have been clearly perceived, ever since the creation of the world, in the things that have been made. So they are without excuse" (Rom 1:20). The unseen character of God is made visible through that which he has made, if we have eyes to see.

CONCLUSION

In Wendell Berry's book on race and prejudice, he discusses artistic imagination. Here's what he writes, specifically mentioning his friend, the novelist Ernest Gaines:

> [Gaines] is not the first in the Western tradition to think of imagination as the means, in any of the arts, whether writing or painting or carpentry or farming, of joining human work rightly to the work of God. To take him seriously is to see in his work an effort to understand and to bring within reach of imagination the meaning of human wholeness, which certainly would involve and even require that joining of the low and the high: earth and heaven, the human neighborhood and the kingdom of God, health and

---

22. Bell, *Meaning of Blue*, 150–51.

holiness. The realization of this wholeness has been the supreme task, always verging on failure, of the lineage of traditional artists.[23]

Here, Berry uses profoundly sacramental language—connecting the low and the high, joining human work to the work of God. This imagination is the work of artists.

A sacramental vision requires a contemplative spirit. An artist with an over-spiritualist imagination might make art that neglects the difficulties of life, turning a blind eye to hardships or injustices. This stems from a "when-we-all-get-to-heaven" mentality that risks conveying an attitude of "just get over it" and leaves no room for lamenting. In this case, meaning can often overshadow the forms. The things of life can be seen as obstacles, and so, rather than leaning into our circumstances with expectation, we turn aside from them in an attempt to overcome them.

To the other extreme, materialists value things only as they appear. This can invite commiseration around the circumstances of life with little acknowledgment of meaning that could be gained in and through the situations we experience in our earthly lives. The intense focus on forms can overshadow anything meaningful to be gained. This lends itself to a formalistic way that emphasizes the medium without regard to a corresponding message.

The early mystic Dionysius suggested that *everything* is a symbol. For Dionysius, the whole cosmos is a theophany, "a manifestation of God in creaturely form, both spiritual and material."[24] This way of seeing the world serves as a constant source of inspiration that, when it is embraced, results in an artistic practice that reaches a new level of richness. This depth compels observers to consider the world as full of deeper meaning, not by way of overt representation, but through an inviting portrayal of the literal that suggests there is meaning beyond what is seen at first glance.

A sacramental imagination leans into life. Rather than sidestepping the joy and pain as barriers, these real aspects of life become necessary, but not ultimate. By contemplation, artists can see the world as integrative and thus display holistic and healing art for the world to look and see.

23. Berry, *Need to Be Whole*, 337.

24. Louth, "Beauty Will Save the World," 69.

Historical Practice: The Oxford Movement and Victorian Artists

ONE OF OUR MAIN influences and dialogue partners is the Oxford Movement, led by John Keble, Edward Pusey, and John Henry Newman in the nineteenth century. What follows is a brief introduction that we will extend throughout the book.

While the Oxford Movement did not set out to inspire a renewal of the arts in Victorian England, the movement did play a significant role in introducing new life into the creative world. This nineteenth-century movement was intended to revive what they considered to be a stagnant English church. The Oxford Movement theologians had largely attributed the state of the church to an over-rational approach to Scripture that had made its way to England from Germany. This way of interpreting Scripture flattened the Bible, valuing it primarily for the knowledge that could be gained through intellectual means alone. A studious approach replaced the prayerful reading of the text. In response, the Oxford theologians advocated for the retrieval of a "typical" reading of the Bible that had been common to the church fathers. They believed this way of interpretation would help the church regain its imagination, renewing its sense of God's nearness.

This ancient hermeneutic has a sacramental character that takes into account the preexistence of Christ, which heightened an awareness of Christ's presence in the Old Testament. Prophecy was not valued only for how it points forward to Christ, but for how it demonstrates all things as participating in him, the Eternal Word. This interpretive practice is an exercise of the imagination that requires the reader to discern Jesus' presence throughout the whole Bible—reading Old Testament figures, events, or rituals as both pointing toward the coming Christ and patterned after Jesus, who preexisted Scripture. The incarnation sets forth a model for the early fathers' interpretation of Scripture, which the Tractarians extended to include creation, arguing that knowledge of God was mediated through flesh, and therefore, God makes himself present to us in the things that he has made. They considered nature to be part of a whole sacramental system—earthly types that signify invisible spiritual truths in various ways and to different degrees.[1]

The Tractarians, which is another name of the Oxford Movement because of the "tracts" they produced, believed that this search for Christ in Scripture would condition the church to see Christ in the world. They believed that an increased awareness of divine activity in creation would help overcome the view of God as remote or impassive. Creation provides us with a sense of God's nearness that is experienced through our enjoyment of nature's combined beauty and function. The mystery the Tractarians sought to recover is grounded in beauty—not that beauty simply leads to a greater admiration of natural forms, but that it serves as an invitation to contemplate the divine presence as it is made known through creation.

The Tractarians suggested that the appeal to reason had stifled the imagination of the church, leading people to understand God as passive. Edward Pusey, a central figure in the movement, observed that a scholastic approach to the Bible sought to explain the literal rather than discover the spiritual meaning in Scripture. Biographer Henry Liddon recalls Pusey's impression of what he termed "new" theology after his visit to study rationalism firsthand in Germany. Liddon writes, "He appreciated the historical and critical information, but felt like these dimensions were primary, and the religious element was subordinate to these. Miracles were explained away, and it was as if the supernatural was insignificant."[2] The Oxford Movement confronted this approach, striving to recover mystery in order to inspire reverence, while also providing an awareness of Christ's presence. They believed that this way of seeing could lead to a spiritual awakening in the English church.

The Oxford theologians recognized that rational arguments were often well-intentioned, meant to inspire faith in an unbeliever. However, the attempt to provide reasonable explanations for the transcendent realities in Scripture often resulted in an unfortunate aversion to mystery. Ironically, even though many explanations for God were intended to inspire faith, they often left skeptics without the need for faith. John Henry Newman described rationalism as "a limiting of the possible to the actual, and denying

---

1. Pusey, "Scriptural Views of Holy Baptism," 272.
2. Liddon, *Life of Pusey*, 1.70.

the indefinite range of God's operations beyond our means of apprehending them."[3] A rationalist approach to gaining knowledge is limited to the study of superficial appearances or the literal meaning of Scripture. However, the evidence used to prove God through rational means often neglects the vast mysteries of the faith and the deeper heavenly realities that are discovered beneath images as we see them.

The movement sought to express the way creation acts sacramentally, making Christ present through an appeal to all our senses. In the tract "On the Mysticism Attributed to the Early Fathers of the Church," John Keble highlights the church fathers' desire to discover the figurative meaning in Scripture and the way this interpretive approach develops our understanding of nature. Keble writes, "And visible things seem to bear relation, not only to the fitting up of this world, but also to the setting forth of things invisible, and to furnish a sort of argument of the things which are not seen; according to the saying in the Prophet, The Heavens declare the glory of God, and the firmament sheweth His handywork. That the invisible things of Him are understood by the things which are made."[4]

The symbolic, or sacramental, reading of Scripture led the early church to a broader acknowledgment of the necessity of symbols in forming the Christian life. Hilary Fraser wrote that John Henry Newman and John Keble "came to regard the Church as that new language which Christ has brought us, providing a suitably poetic medium for God's poetic revelation of Himself to man."[5] Ceremonial revival was not the goal of the Tractarians. However, by observing Christ's poetic way of revealing truth, the church began to recover an appreciation for the way literal forms can encourage participation with God in the context of worship, by way of beauty and function. While rationalism often leads toward a disembodied faith, the multisensory aspects of ceremonial worship would inspire a more embodied, participatory experience of God. Beauty became valued for the formative effect it has on the soul by drawing us into its Source.

Churches throughout England had replaced many of the symbolic elements in worship with longer sermons, which the Tractarian Issac Williams thought implied that God could be understood with our minds, therefore, the church began to overlook the need for symbolic means of participation. However, the movement's sacramentality of creation inspired the church to

3. Newman, "On the Introduction of Rationalistic Principles into Religion," 4.
4. Keble, "On the Mysticism Attributed to the Early Fathers of the Church," 6.12.
5. Fraser, *Beauty and Belief*, 32.

examine the role of beauty in drawing us into union with Christ. With this in mind, the church began to summon craftspeople, architects, poets, and more to create symbols that engage the senses and invite worshippers into participation with God. A renewed appreciation for symbolic participation resulted in embodied forms of worship—spoken prayers and enactments of the Word through postures, seeing, smelling, and tasting. Hymnody was revived, surely influenced by a poetic approach to Scripture and life in general. The production of textiles increased during and following the movement, as well as tapestries and vestments, stained glass and liturgical furniture–and it introduced a revival in Gothic architecture in England. Edward Pusey acknowledged the importance of beauty for growth in the Christian life and demonstrated this by subsidizing the building of church-es in the industrial inner cities of England in an attempt to bring beauty to dark or drab places. The church building was seen as an example of the perfect kind of art because it combines beauty and function, encouraging participation and proclaiming the good news using more than words.

The artistic revival extended beyond the walls of churches. We will highlight two artists who display principles adopted from the Oxford Movement. First, the visual art of William Holman Hunt is a primary ex-ample of the way the symbolic, or "typological," reading of the biblical text influenced Victorian artists. Second, Christina Rossetti's poetry models a Tractarian theological method.

John Ruskin declared Holman Hunt's *The Light of the World* to be one of the "noblest works of sacred art produced in this or any other age."[6] This painting exhibits an approach referred to as symbolic realism, a form that is often considered to be the result of the sacramental teaching of the Oxford Movement. In *The Light of the World*, Holman Hunt portrays Jesus almost as if he is a priest in Victorian England. He wears an alb and cope while standing in an English orchard. This painting is an example of the way William Holman Hunt imagines Christ in the present, as if he were here, inviting the viewer to see Christ as being among us. While such a depiction could project Jesus in our own image, the desire of the Oxford Movement was to renew an awareness of the nearness of Jesus throughout all reaches of life.

Holman Hunt was a part of the Pre-Raphaelite Brotherhood, a move-ment that sought to confront the over-romanticized artistic depictions of his day. The Pre-Raphaelite Brotherhood rebelled against English art that

6. Ruskin, *Modern Painters II*, 412.

they considered to be obsessed with form—the perfection of technique, and further, depicted life in an unrealistic manner. The Brotherhood protested a fantastical imagining of Christ that seemed disconnected from earthly life—a representation that appeared to disjoin the heavenly from the earthly, leaving us with no imagination for Christ's presence in the world. Many Pre-Raphaelite Brotherhood artists sought to portray real life, composing relatable art by utilizing familiar imagery. The realistic depictions of Holman Hunt and others in the Brotherhood were often considered to be scandalous and were scrutinized for being irreverent. However, his portrayal of everyday life in Victorian England exhibited his desire to capture real life. His use of layers of meaning, conspicuously hidden within the image, displayed his enchanted vision of the world.

The Oxford Movement's sacramental teaching of the Bible regarded Old Testament images as symbols that find fulfillment in the New Testament (antitypes) or reveal the character of Jesus (the Archetype). George Landow captures the profound influence that this teaching had on Victorian artists, stating, "When we modern readers fail to recognize allusions to such typology, we deprive many Victorian works of a large part of their context."[7] Landow suggests that our capability to understand Victorian art is severely limited when typology is not taken into account. He specifically refers to the typological interpretation that was advocated by Newman and Keble of the Oxford Movement.

Second, Christina Rossetti is the poet most identified with the Oxford Movement's theological principles. The teaching of analogy and reserve, concepts associated with the sacramental reading advocated by Tractarians (and two terms that we will return to and develop later), were impactful for many Victorian artists, including Rossetti—not only influencing their interpretation of Scripture but also their approach to art. The Tractarian basis for analogy stems from the reality that God is the source of both nature and Scripture. Creation holds meaning since it is from God, though its significance is not limited to being a sign that points back to its origin. Tractarian Isaac Williams wrote extensively on the concept of reserve, encouraging restraint when teaching essential doctrines, recognizing the benefit of gradual revelation for instilling faith.[8] He urged a more nuanced and gradual approach toward comprehension and discernment of sacred

7. Landow, *Victorian Types, Victorian Shadows*, 15.

8. Williams, "On Reserve," nos. 80 and 87.

truths, a posture artists are sure to recognize and appreciate, and a trait that runs throughout Christina Rossetti's poetry.

G. B. Tennyson refers to Rossetti as "the true inheritor of the Tractarian mode in poetry."[9] The Tractarian sacramentality of creation has been credited with providing the basis for Rossetti's analogical view of the world and her implementation of nature in poetry as a vehicle of divine truth. Rossetti depicts a sacramental world by using earthly images in the way God has intended: to make the divine presence known through that which he has created. In John Keble's Tract 89, he speaks of the use of analogy in our attempt to make sense of transcendent meaning, stating, "There is everywhere a tendency to make the things we see represent the things we do not see, to invent or remark mutual associations between them, to call the one sort by the names of the other."[10] In her poetry, Christina Rossetti draws upon the analogies of creation as the means to express that which is indescribable, while exercising an appropriate level of restraint, in order to avoid the implication that it is possible to adequately describe God. She incorporates these analogies into her poetry just as she observes them, as an indirect means of revealing truths that are too great for words. By pointing to the analogies in nature, she models a way of seeing; as an artist, she invites us to see the world through her eyes, and in doing so, she makes a profound statement about God's mode of communicating truth.

The restraint that Rossetti uses is a characteristic of the concept of reserve, which was central to the effort set forth by the Oxford Movement to preserve reverence and mystery. As a result of this teaching, she pursued a subtle way of speaking about divine truths, using analogy as a means of gradual revelation in her writing. Rossetti found it presumptuous to do for God what he has chosen not to do himself, which is to use nature to reveal himself in obvious ways. By implementing reserve, Rossetti leaves revelation to God as he determines, rather than presume that she has the authority to reveal spiritual truths on his behalf. David Shaw speaks of her process, saying, "In a group of lyrics envisaging the end of the world, the end of the poet's life, and the darkness of God, Rossetti tries to familiarize mystery by imposing upon it the comfort of limit. But in order to hold meaning in reserve and keep alive a mute sense of strangeness Rossetti is continually extending or breaking down the limits she imposes."[11] This statement ex-

---

9. Tennyson, *Victorian Devotional Poetry*, 201.

10. Keble, "On the Mysticism Attributed to the Early Fathers of the Church," 6.4.

11. Shaw, "Poet of Mystery," 40.

presses the discernment she uses when speaking of divine things, which is a reflection of her reverence for God and the unexplainable mysteries that imbue creation. She displays humility in her method, acknowledging her dependence on God for understanding the profound vastness of his being.

While we get a glimpse of the vastness of God, the vastness is to be approached with reverence and not mastery. Along the same lines, in the tract "On Reserve in Communicating Religious Knowledge," Isaac Williams states,

> In things natural, God has not only disclosed to us, by experience and natural light, the mode of tilling the earth and all other things necessary for the support of our animal life and human comforts, but he has also afforded us some knowledge of the heavenly bodies; He has withdrawn the veil and opened something of the mysterious vastness, and ways, and order of things celestial. And in disclosing these, there is of course some great design of His Providence towards men; whether to humble them by showing something of the vastness of His power, or to raise and spiritualize their minds by the contemplation of it.[12]

Understanding is a provision where God gifts us with glimpses of "mysterious vastness." This experience humbles the one who contemplates, knowing that this vision is much bigger than what they can conjure up alone.

Likewise, Edward Pusey recognized understanding was a gift from God. In other words, a sacramental imagination cannot come from human effort alone but requires us to pursue holiness, to know God by identifying with Christ in our obedience. Pusey referred to poets as moral philosophers who trace out "the mutual correspondence between image and reality."[13] Drawing out these associations requires sight that comes from God. This mode of discovery, or drawing out meaning, is contrasted with the common practice of projecting meaning upon an object to represent an idea or feeling. Pusey refers to the primary role of the poet to *discover* an actual meaning, rather than *inventing* a fictional likeness of God. The Tractarians understood God to communicate poetically through nature, and it was assumed that artists would likewise use analogies to poetically reveal truth.

These statements put sight, the ability to perceive the things of God, as the primary goal of artists. In fact, this way of discernment is described as a

12. Williams, "On Reserve," 4.8.
13. Pusey, "Lectures on Types and Prophecies," 16.

poetical act, one that requires us to recognize God's means of communication and then to consider what truth is held within the analogies. This way of seeing takes cooperation with God in order to recognize where he is made known and then to faithfully reveal what we discover. We have much to learn from the teaching of the Oxford Movement. Artists could benefit from the movement's sacramental vision of creation, but these benefits are not associated with technique or form; rather, they begin with learning how to see.

5

Reading Scripture and Reading Our Lives: On Symbolism, Signs, and Analogy

In a symbolical universe, everything is in its proper place because everything answers to everything else. In such a harmonious system, the serpent is homogeneous with the virtue of prudence; and yet the same serpent can symbolise Satan. It was a kind of polyphony of signs and references. Christ and His divinity were symbolised by a vast number and variety of creatures, each signifying His presence in a different place—in heaven, on mountain-tops, in the fields, the forests, and the seas. The symbols used included the lamb, the dove, the peacock, the ram, the gryphon, the rooster, the lynx, the palm-tree, even a bunch of grapes: a polyphony of images.

—UMBERTO ECO

Even though Your symbol may be small,
Yet it is a fountain of further mysteries.

—ST. EPHRAIM THE SYRIAN

For Seeking God   *Anselm of Canterbury*

Teach me to seek you, and as I seek you, show yourself to me; for I cannot seek you unless you show me how, and I will never find you unless you show yourself to me. Let me seek you by desiring you, and desire you by seeking you; let me find you by loving you, and love you in finding you. Amen.

IN THE BEGINNING, GOD created. These first words of the Bible clue us in to something fundamental about the divine being: he is a Creator. As Makoto Fujimura points out, "God the Artist communicates to us first, before God the lecturer."[1] God unveils himself to us as a poet. He then goes on speaking the world into existence. He begins with a poem about the creation of the world and the creation of man and woman. In this divine poem, God's words become realities. There is something both spiritual (the words spoken) and material (the stuff created). Each created thing reveals something about the truth, goodness, and beauty of the Creator. In his introduction to *Christ: The Sacramental Word,* David Brown states, "Words are more than sounds; they are signs and symbols pointing beyond themselves, mediating the reality into which they draw us."[2] Brown claims that Word and flesh function sacramentally, one participating in the other.

Because of this artistic foundation, the church fathers and mothers approached the Bible in imaginative rather than a purely rationalistic way. They approached the Bible aesthetically, creatively, and artistically. They were referred to as poets, or even as artists, because of their particular reading of Scripture. They interpreted the Bible in a poetic manner and exposited the text in beautiful ways, drawing associations between the literal meaning and the spiritual realities veiled therein. In interpreting Scripture, the church fathers and mothers weren't necessarily after "the one" meaning so often pursued in modern hermeneutics. Rather, they were after God's presence. They wanted communion more than they wanted answers. Many took an allegorical approach that came as a result of the sacramental principles they had observed in the incarnation of Christ. The incarnation also provided the basis for their understanding of the sacraments, especially the correspondence between the material forms and spiritual benefits. Further, this principle was carried over into their understanding of the revelation of God in creation. Their approach to Scripture, the sacraments, and creation was based on their principle that each of these forms was symbolically referring to something beyond itself. They considered the Old Testament to be an example of the way God communicates according to the way humans learn.

Due to the limitation of human rationality, God chooses to communicate through symbols. Hans Urs von Balthasar refers to the insufficiency of our imagination, quoting Maximus the Confessor, "To comprehend

1. Fujimura, *Art+Faith,* 7.
2. Brown and Loades, eds., "Introduction," 4.

accurately even the least of creatures is beyond the power of our reason."[3] The use of symbolism takes into account the inability of humans to perceive God through the use of intellect alone. Furthermore, the use of symbols throughout the Bible demonstrates God's desire for us to experience his presence in various ways by appealing to all our senses. Thus, as interpreters and artists, we need a creative approach to interpretation, which will require a prayerful and contemplative posture. Not all of us will be mystics, but we can be aided by a mystical approach to discover truth that may not be apparent on the surface.

To think that we can capture the full essence of God in a word or image is to fool ourselves into thinking that God can be reduced to the confines of the imagination. Nevertheless, our search to know him continues as we strive to interpret the world in light of our yearning for the transcendent. For now, we are left with symbols—created means that are given to us to convey what God is "like." Symbols, in a limited way, say something of the divine. And so, to various degrees, God does make himself seen, and in light of this revelation, we can draw from God's own analogies to reflect his character in our art. The early church demonstrated the way a poetic reading of Scripture leads to a poetic understanding of all of life. By seeking Christ in Old Testament symbols, for example, they became accustomed to seeing all creation as symbolic, which reveals the nearness of Christ in all things.

SCRIPTURE, SYMBOLS, AND SIGNS

The expectancy of seeing Christ in the world led the church fathers and mothers toward a distinct way of reading the biblical text. Their interpretation of Scripture had a symbolic character that was the result of their belief that the Old Testament points back to Christ as the preexistent Word and prophetically points forward to the future incarnation. This dynamic means that because Christ was before all things, they read the text with an awareness that every event, person, or ritual in the Old Testament bore his fingerprints. With this in mind, they read with an understanding that Christ can be seen throughout the whole Bible.

The theophany in Exodus 33 offers an example of the fathers' imaginative way of reading the biblical text. In his work on *The Trinity*, the fourth-century bishop St. Augustine challenges us to consider that everywhere

3. Balthasar, *Cosmic Liturgy*, 91.

God appears in the Old Testament, Christ is also there. He points to Exodus 33, referring to God allowing Moses to see his back as calling attention to flesh, his physical presence, and therefore, is a reference to Christ. He adds that the rock on which Moses stood must represent the church because it is only from this place that one can safely look upon the Lord. St. Augustine's comments on this Old Testament story derive from his understanding that the visions "were produced through the changeable creation subject to the changeless God, and they did not manifest God as he is in himself, but in a symbolic manner as times and circumstances required."[4] Here, St. Augustine displays a redemptively symbolic manner of reading Scripture. He does not intend to add meaning to the text; instead, he demonstrates the richness of the text as he prayerfully looks beyond the literal reading to discover the presence of Christ. As noted by Alejandro García-Rivera, "Augustine's anagogy . . . was a movement within Creation not one that takes us out of Creation . . . Augustine's anagogy has the rudimentary structure of a theory of a sign, i.e. a visible signifier standing for an invisible signified."[5] It was St. Augustine's training and desire to see Christ in the Old Testament that allowed him to find him there.

Referring to this same Old Testament story in Exodus 33 in *The Life of Moses*, St. Gregory of Nyssa states that the very suggestion of God having a body leads the interpreter to conclude that there must be meaning beyond the literal reading because God does not have an incorruptible and incorporeal body. With this in mind, he begins to read symbolically, drawing associations between the real occurrence in its context with the New Testament revelation of Christ and his church. St. Gregory proclaims that Moses' soul was lifted up by his desire to see God, stating, "Hope always draws the soul from the beauty which is seen to what is beyond, always kindles the desire for the hidden through what is constantly perceived."[6] He contends that the mountain Moses ascended was literal, but further symbolized the manner in which his understanding and desire to see and know God began to ascend. Gregory writes, "In speaking of a 'place' he does not limit the place indicated by anything quantitative (for something to be non-quantitative there is no measure). On the contrary, using the analogy of a measurable surface he leads the hearer to the unlimited and infinite."[7] He

4. Augustine, *The Trinity*, 124.

5. García-Rivera, *Community of the Beautiful*, 30.

6. As quoted in Foltz, *Medieval Philosophy*, 114.

7. As quoted in Foltz, *Medieval Philosophy*, 117.

equates the measurable and quantitative rock in this Old Testament story to the immeasurable reality of Christ, who is steadfast and unmovable. Again, Gregory does not add meaning to the text but draws out the symbols that are already present in the story. Gregory encourages readers to engage with the text, reminding us that Christ is discovered within the literal reading if we have eyes to see.

The allegorical reading of Scripture as exhibited here by Augustine and Gregory is not formulaic; it isn't intended to be a methodical approach for interpreting the Bible. Instead, it appears to be a natural consequence of their sacramental imagination, a consistent model that informs both biblical interpretation and the understanding of the way God is revealed in creation. This approach to Scripture is an example of the way spiritual perception informs our understanding of all things. While it is true that the church fathers' symbolic reading of the Bible *formed* their sacramental understanding of earthly forms, it could also be argued that this way of interpretation is *a consequence* of their sacramental understanding of creation. Their reading of Scripture and their view of the world is reciprocal in this regard. Regardless of which came first, both exhibit a sacramentality that pervades their thinking, fueled by their desire to experience Christ's presence.

On occasion, the fathers' reading of the Old Testament might appear fanciful, or a bit over the top; however, the connections they make are the result of their quest to discern Christ everywhere in the Bible. If Christ is "before all things," then the events of the Old Testament not only point toward Jesus but are patterned after him. It makes sense that if Christ pre-existed before creation, then his character must be reflected in all that is made. Furthermore, the preexistence of Jesus inspired them to draw associations between the Old Testament and Christ—they sought him everywhere and found him in the wood of Noah's ark, the waters of the Red Sea, and the rock that Moses stood upon.

While the Enlightenment required evidence for God by looking at literal and historical information, the fathers were after something different. Spiritual understanding cannot be obtained from surface realities alone but understanding is mined from the various layers of meaning that sometimes rest beneath the literal level. David Brown has remarked, "Yet in marked contrast to sixteenth- and seventeenth-century translators of the Bible, our modern preoccupation equates accuracy with the elimination of ambiguity, with narrowing (no doubt, sometimes rightly) the possible range of meanings. It suggests a less meditative, less engaged way of reading the text."[8] This meditative and engaged reading is what Scripture inspires. The Bible is poetic, requiring contemplation—like reading poetry rather than a textbook.

James Taylor is an education philosopher who compares scientific knowledge to poetic knowledge. He describes poetic knowledge as a "sensory-emotional" knowledge of what is really there. It's not made-up or subjective but it's responsive to an embodied reality beyond the head. He compares this type of knowledge to scientific knowledge by using Charles Dickens's novel *Hard Times*. The fictional professor Thomas Gradgrind wants Facts: "Now, what I want is Facts. Teach these boys and girls nothing but Facts. Facts alone are wanted in life. Plant nothing else. You can only form the minds of reasoning animals upon Facts: nothing else will ever be of any service to them."[9] How many of us have been raised with this sort of education? In regard to the Bible, we've been formed to look at Facts, as if Scripture interpretation was just a glorified AWANA Bible quiz. Rather than this scientific knowledge, poetic knowledge does not objectify things by abstract facts but enters into the real. This kind of knowledge, Taylor goes on, results from "the *love* of a thing, person, or place."[10] Poetic knowledge stems from love, and this love dictates Scripture interpretation, and for the sake of this book, the artistic task. Love is primary in how we know and see the world. Love inspires wonder and delight rather than mastery.

Rational explanations for transcendent realities always fall short. Historical or scientific conclusions alone are insufficient. Therefore, God uses symbolism to reveal that which words cannot express. We should note that literal forms do not exist apart from that which they are made to reveal. On using metaphors symbolically, David Brown states, "The symbolism of the metaphor reinforces the symbolism of the sacramental reality, enriching it such that word, far from simplifying the act, actually adds further layers of intensity of reference to whatever is enacted during the course of the sacrament's celebration."[11] These layers of intensity are what is meant by a sacramental reality being symbolic. Latent within symbols are revelations of meaning, thus enhancing and enriching the symbolic object.

8. Brown and Loades, eds., "Introduction," 11.

9. Dickens, *Hard Times*, 3.

10. Taylor, *Poetic Knowledge*, 7.

11. Brown and Loades, eds., "Introduction," 17.

Likewise, the poet Malcolm Guite argues that meaning is not a human invention. Drawing on a discussion of Samuel Taylor Coleridge, Guite suggests that the meaning of objects "is a symbol, but is not a randomly chosen or arbitrarily constructed human symbol. It is a symbol that is given, is moulded by and participates in the reality it represents."[12] There's a givenness to symbol that is not a result of human ingenuity. Coleridge himself adds, "The Symbol is characterized by . . . the translucence of the Eternal through and in the Temporal. It always partakes of the Reality which it renders intelligible; and while it enunciates the whole, abides itself as a living part in that Unity, of which it is representative."[13] Symbolic language is filled with such sacramental explanations—the translucence of the eternal through and in the temporal.

ALLEGORY AND ANALOGY

Allegory is an example of the way language can function in a symbolic, or sacramental, way. Allegory refers to a means of interpretation that considers the real elements of a story to be symbols that are meant to convey an idea by pointing beyond itself. In a biblical sense, allegory is not meant to imply that the symbols are useless except for the meaning that is communicated; rather, the literal forms are necessary, and deeply related to the reality to which they point. David Brown states, "(Words) mediate the reality into which they draw us." He refers to the sacramental character of words, according to Emily Dickinson, saying, "She characterizes all words as seeking to enable us to participate in something beyond themselves."[14] Allegory exemplifies the participatory nature of the sacramentality of creation by using words to invite us to contemplate the correspondence between a symbol and the thing it represents.

The term "allegory" carries with it some intellectual baggage in modern Christianity. To say something is "allegorical" often implies that something is fake or made up, but the opposite is true. Just as material is a necessary component of the sacrament, the literal remains an essential part of allegorical interpretation. As Benjamin Myers urges, "Real allegory depends on the literal in order to reach the symbolic."[15] The people, ritu-

12. Guite, *Faith, Hope and Poetry*, 158.

13. Coleridge, "Statesman's Manual," 30–31.

14. Brown and Loades, eds., "Introduction," 4.

15. Myers, *Poetics of Orthodoxy*, 91.

als, and events of the Old Testament maintain their temporal value in an allegorical reading of Scripture. In fact, the literal forms have more meaning given the divine purpose for which they were made.

Poets draw upon earthly images to communicate when words fail to adequately describe transcendent realities, using nature as symbolic representations of higher truths. These natural images often recall that which is hidden or concealed, and occasionally challenge readers to reimagine their perception of familiar forms. The poet understands that images communicate deep truths in ways that overt explanations cannot. In his *Lectures on Poetry*, John Keble states, "[Poetry's] chief aim is to recall, to renew, and bring vividly before us pictures of absent objects: partly it has to draw out and bring to light things cognate or similar to each object it represents, however slight the connection may be."[16] This is exactly what the fathers were enacting in their interpretation of the Old Testament, and likely the reason Keble suggested that they functioned as true poets by "making the unseen world perceptible to man."[17]

The concept of an *analogy* provides a link between the way we read Scripture and our vision of creation. Analogies are a key component of allegorical reading, where surface realities are symbolic of an underlying meaning. "Allegorical" interpretation is also referred to as spiritual, mystical, or symbolic. These descriptive terms all point to analogy as an essential way of communicating truths that are beyond explanation. In *The Divine Names* Dionysius uses the terms "symbols" and "analogies" interchangeably. He states, "And so it is that the Transcendent is clothed in terms of being, with shape and form on things which have neither, and numerous symbols are employed to convey the varied attributes of what is an imageless and supra-natural simplicity." Dionysius then explains that symbols are used for the things of God, and "with these analogies we are raised upwards toward the truth of the mind's vision."[18] He refers to the way God mediates himself to us through the senses, and thus believes symbolic revelation, "types," to be essential. Paul Rorem comments, "The realm of symbols is not merely an optional means through which one may be elevated; it is the only means."[19] We see in this statement God's commitment to the symbolic role of creation in uplifting the mind. Symbols, by nature, point beyond

16. Keble, *Lectures on Poetry*, 21.

17. Prickett, *Romanticism and Religion*, 117.

18. Dionysius, "Divine Names," 52–53.

19. Rorem, *Biblical and Liturgical Symbols*, 105.

themselves. We move through them—our understanding of God ascends through our interaction with perceptible forms. God is seen in creation, and through it we gain a portion of the vision of God. Eric Perl writes, "The unknowable God is known only in the structure of the created world."[20] This analogical understanding of the world made early Christian interpreters see the world symbolically.

Analogy is frequently thought of as a way of simplifying an obscure idea by comparing it to an unrelated, yet similar form. However, analogies are not a figment of the imagination, as if meaning is projected onto an object to make a comparison. They are not conjured in the mind of each individual interpreter. Instead, analogies are drawn out of creation, suggesting that a corresponding meaning *already* exists and is discerned as we grow to have eyes to see.

In this sense, art is naturally symbolic because it will always contain a deeper meaning. When we are attentive and available to God's purpose, the body of our creative activity will always come from and ultimately point to a place of hope, of grace. This should not imply that art is contrived, the result of a desperate grasping for meaning, but it is to say that artistic representation should have a natural depth due to its origin. Artistic expression should flow freely from our experience of the world, though it isn't always simple or without effort. In fact, this way of seeing might even require more from artists.

J. R. R. Tolkien can be used as an exemplar of such sacramental symbolism. In *Tolkien's Sacramental Vision*, Craig Bernthal states that Tolkien sought to create a sacramental text that "refers to and participates in a reality greater than itself. It does not take an idea and then invent a material reality to express it, but works through the material to represent a greater truth."[21] Bernthal reminds us that real life has a meaning beyond itself; we live in a God-filled world. He refers to the sacrament as being a particular kind of symbol, "referring to and participating in a divine reality greater than itself."[22] To this end Tolkien aspired to be symbolic in a sacramental sense, relying on creation to point back to the Creator. He depends on the model of interpretation that relies on the divine for spiritual perception to draw out meaning that all nature has to offer in different degrees and in a variety of ways. Furthermore, as Bernthal argues, Tolkien's use of analogy

20. Perl, "Symbol, Sacrament, and Hierarchy," 315.
21. Bernthal, *Tolkien's Sacramental Vision*, 33.
22. Bernthal, *Tolkien's Sacramental Vision*, 32.

can be seen in his robust description of the landscape, which requires "his work to be read at a walking pace to appreciate its beauty."[23] Tolkien uses nature sacramentally to suggest that spiritual meaning is not found outside or apart from the natural but is entered into through the material world. However, grasping the transcendent qualities in Tolkien's work requires contemplation, an almost immersive participation with the text, in order to decipher the corresponding realities. Bernthal describes the world from which Tolkien operated, stating, "The Catholic universe is not Gnostic, but Incarnational, and God is not only transcendent, but immanent."[24] This is the reason Tolkien can appeal to the analogies found in nature, not only to act as a sign that points to a particular meaning, but to allow nature to speak from its very character. With this in mind, Bernthal reminds us that Tolkien makes the reader feel as if the soil and trees of the Shire are full of grace. His intertwining of the spiritual realities with natural images provides us with the opportunity to discern meaning that differs and is revealed in accordance with the reader's ability to perceive. Tolkien's use of analogy preserves a sense of mystery with an ever-present presence of something more than what is gleaned from a surface reading.

In many ways, Tolkien is putting flesh to St. Paul's explanation of the revelatory role of creation, that God intends for us to learn from the analogies found in nature. In Romans 1:20, Paul writes, "For his invisible attributes, namely, his eternal power and divine nature, have been clearly perceived, ever since the creation of the world, in the things that have been made." Edward Pusey describes the various aspects of creation as rungs on a ladder through which we ascend toward God. Pusey states, "The tendency of all things toward God, is, as in an image set forth, in the tendency of all things to meet together in unity." Quoting Francis Bacon, Pusey continues, "that all things as by a ladder rise up to unity."[25] This view of analogy suggests that nature has been purposefully made to draw us into the life of God. The analogy of creation isn't something that exists separate from God but by being what it was made to be, nature participates with God for this purpose. This relationship expresses the sacramental nature of a symbol.

23. Bernthal, *Tolkien's Sacramental Vision*, 22.
24. Bernthal, *Tolkien's Sacramental Vision*, 22.
25. Pusey, "Lectures on Types and Prophecies," 18.

ALLEGORY AND ART

Here's our contention in this book: If God is the Artist who communicates to us poetically, then we image God by poetically seeing and then shaping the world in which we find ourselves. We want to make the continual appeal that artists cannot segment their lives. Our vision should affect and be affected by how we see Scripture, the world, the sacraments, our relationships, and our art. We're after a holistic and healthy imagination. As we seek to understand the mysteries of God through the things he has made, we come to inherit his poetic way of communicating. A symbol communicates differently than a sign in that there is a real correspondence between the material symbol and that which it reveals. Rather than pointing to something other than itself like a sign, symbols participate in the things they point to. Therefore, by participating with that symbol, we are drawn into the life of the One it was made to represent. A symbol is sacramental in that it invites participation with the real.

By understanding symbols and allegories in Scripture, artists can see the world in symbolic and analogical ways and create from such a vision. Analogy, words or images, are used as an indirect mode of conveying heavenly realities. Analogy facilitates a gradual manner of revelation as God sees fit. This way of communication sets forth a model that relieves artists of the pressure to provide adequate explanations for inexpressible mysteries. Artists offer their work back to God when they utilize forms as subtle, indirect references to transcendent realities—trusting divine truth to be revealed as he desires. However, because the divine is not inherently contained within a created object, it is possible for natural symbols to be interpreted in a variety of ways. When the weight of interpretation is placed on viewing art through spiritual eyes, differing interpretations should be expected. Symbols tend to work in this manner, especially when there is not a "one-to-one" correspondence between an image and a specific truth. George MacDonald writes, "For in everything that God has made, there is layer upon layer of ascending significance."[26] Likewise, art often has layer upon layer of ascending significance. When we use God's things in our expressions, we might even stumble upon those who draw meaning from our work that we had never intended. MacDonald refers to the way God uses the work of an artist almost as a natural consequence of our desire to take hold of higher meaning. He states, "A man may well himself discover truth

26. MacDonald, *Gifts of the Child Christ*, 27.

in what he wrote; for he was dealing all the time with things that came from thoughts beyond his own."[27]

A sacramental imagination can be cultivated in artists as we grow to understand the way God uses earthly forms in symbolic ways. God draws us into participation through our interaction with his creation, and when artists gain a clearer vision of veiled spiritual realities, they become more proficient at inviting observers into participation with that which they imitate. A sacramental vision of creation is an important aspect of life in Christ and is especially meaningful for artists who recognize their primary role as reflecting the glory of God. Artists often represent the world in a symbolic, or analogical way. Therefore, a central task of artists is to attempt to understand the way God uses natural forms in a symbolic manner.

David Jones, a contemporary English artist, refers to artists as signmakers—something we suggested in alluding to artists as sacramental iconographers. Jones insists, "The artist deals wholly in signs."[28] His claim is that religion and art share signs in common. He describes signs as sacramental, partaking in God, as opposed to simply pointing to him. Jones writes, "Things that are the signs of something other, together with those signs that not only have the nature of a sign but are themselves, under some mode, what they signify."[29] He uses baptism as an example, relating the familiar language associated with baptismal water to poetically describe the water that surrounds the British Isles. By making this correlation, he indicates how the sentimental relationship with water in the islanders' everyday life is used to draw their minds to the spiritual waters of baptism. Being a sign-maker requires the artist to connect familiar forms, or even memories, to a spiritual sentiment—deeper, heavenly meaning. There is no shortage of images or types, and as Jones suggests, we use these forms (which are for our use), to represent the stories they have been made by God to tell. In this sense, artists are not sign-makers as much as we are sign-readers. This, Jones states, is the specific task of the artist.

As much as we may agree with Jones, there is often a reticence among Christians to incorporate glimpses of heavenly meaning in their work. This hesitation seems to be rooted in a belief that art is cheapened when a spiritual component is purposefully included and thus considered to be functional.

27. MacDonald, *Complete Fairy Tales*, 9.
28. Jones, *Anathemata*, 15.
29. Jones, *Anathemata*, 29.

Cultural analyst, sociologist, and philosopher Jean Baudrillard is often critical of modern artists' efforts to separate meaning from their art. He laments the way in which art is frequently described by what it is *not*, rather than what it *is*. Baudrillard states, "Art, in its form, signifies nothing. It is only a sign of absence."[30] For Baudrillard, this hollow expression reflects a pervasive modern view of the universe as emptied of meaning. He quips, "It turned this uselessness into a reason for praise. By extension of this principle, making any object useless would be enough to make it a work of art. This is precisely what the ready made does when it merely divests itself of its function, without changing anything about it, to turn it into a museum piece. It is sufficient to make reality itself a useless function to turn it into an art object, prey to the all-consuming aesthetic of banality."[31] Baudrillard argues that a deconstructed *view* of the world is to blame for the rise of deconstructed art, which he then suggests deconstructs the viewer. The credence he gives to the formational (and/or deformational) effect of art upon an observer suggests that a symbolic view and artistic representation of the world has the potential to form the vision of those who interact with it. It is possible that by contemplating the layers of meaning in a particular work of art, the vision of both the artist and spectator is being conditioned.

If it is true that art can play a role in forming sacramental vision, then the Christian artist uniquely participates with God in revealing important yet hidden truths. We would argue that artists are predisposed to interpreting the world symbolically; they seem to think about images more figuratively, contemplating the way a form functions to represent an invisible meaning. This vision is a subtle mode of communication that requires contemplation.

It is common for artists to appreciate subtlety, and even to notice the obscure ways that figures or colors convey meaning beyond their appearance. Referring to Gerard Manley Hopkins's view of nature, John Riches writes, "The creative springing up of things within them which gives them their individual form which holds them and which it is the poet's task to read and to discern, for it is here that we discern, directly as it were, the creative work of God."[32] It was Hopkins who wrote, "I do not think I have ever seen anything more beautiful than the bluebell I have been looking at. I know the beauty of our Lord by it." Perhaps the eye of an artist is

30. Baudrillard, *Conspiracy of Art*, 93.
31. Baudrillard, *Conspiracy of Art*, 95.
32. Riches, "Balthasar's Sacramental Spirituality," 176.

conditioned to seek hidden meaning in creation, and as God wills it, to interpret spiritual meaning that is veiled by nature. Ideally, through their work, artists will train others to see created forms in a similar manner—as symbols of deeper truths, and as a result, those who contemplate their art will begin to perceive the nearness of God.

O'CONNOR AND ROSSETTI AS SACRAMENTAL MODELS

In what follows, we employ the examples of Flannery O'Connor and Christina Rossetti as exemplars of poetic imagination through allegory and symbolism. Their works incorporate metaphor and analogy sacramentally: material, real objects that point to spiritual, invisible realities. This adds layers of depth to their art. Analogy bids the observer to contemplate in order to discover a deeper meaning.

Flannery O'Connor's spiritual vision results in an artistic expression that is sacramental. She doesn't set out to make sacramental art, but her vision clearly influences her writing. O'Connor suggests, "I think that for the fiction writer himself, symbols are something he uses simply as a matter of course. You might say that these are details that, while having their essential place in the literal level of the story, operate in depth as well as on the surface, increasing the story in every direction."[33] She acknowledges the necessity of the literal to mediate truth through the senses. The literal becomes a symbol that allows meaning to unfold over time, participation with the figures and characters in her stories enable a slow unveiling of the layers of truth contained within.

In her short story "Good Country People," one of the main characters, Hulga, has a wooden leg. Throughout the story we see the wooden leg, an earthly form, begins to represent meaning that goes beyond its physical role. O'Connor says, "If you want to say that the wooden leg is a symbol, you can say that. But it is a wooden leg first and as a wooden leg, it is absolutely necessary to the story. It has its place on the literal level of the story, but it operates in depth as well as on the surface."[34] This statement displays her understanding of the essential role of the literal as an instrument that reveals deeper meaning. This does not devalue the importance of the wooden leg, but it gives it more meaning by the nature of the truth it was made to deliver. It functions sacramentally: pointing beyond itself.

33. O'Connor, *Mystery and Manners*, 71.
34. O'Connor, *Mystery and Manners*, 99.

O'Connor did not start writing a story with a message in mind and then look for an appropriate symbol to deliver that meaning. Instead, the forms she used began taking on meaning as the story progressed. She states that the wooden leg *accumulates* meaning. For instance, Hulga is "spiritually as well as crippled physically. There is a wooden part of her soul that corresponds to her wooden leg." O'Connor is careful to add, "now of course it's never stated."[35] This brief statement displays her understanding of the role of a symbol as an earthly form that often veils a meaning that requires the discernment of the reader. This is what a sacramental vision does—it leads us to discern the correspondence between earthly and heavenly realities and then to faithfully display them in our art.

The work of Victorian poet Christina Rossetti provides another fitting example of how an analogical view of the world influences art. While there are moments that Rossetti imposes meaning upon creation to provide helpful comparisons, it is more common for Rossetti to discover meaning through contemplating nature, then she uses the image as a means of revealing. In "The Trees' Counselling," Rossetti admires the contentment of the tree, which, by being what it is, reveals to her a divine lesson. She concludes, "Go not from it as it found thee/ Turn thyself and gaze around thee."[36] Here, Rossetti does not add meaning to the tree but discovers the contentment that this tree has displayed simply by being what it is. She's invited into a sacred participation by seeing how ordinary things exist according to their holy design.

Further, in "Where neither rust nor moth doth corrupt," she draws from Scripture and nature, as she prays to be more like the swallow than the sparrow. Rossetti longs to be content (like the swallow), to remain where she is, yet eager to respond when called to go. Joel Westerholm writes, "She learns, analogically, that she should be like the swallow, unbound by what she has so that she is ready to migrate, not to the south, but to a world beyond 'this deathstruck life and deathlier evil.'"[37] Rossetti's poetry frequently reflects her sacramental view of creation: the tree is really there but communicates beyond the tree itself. God is teaching her a spiritual lesson about contentment through the material object. In the same way that God uses earthly forms to analogically convey a deeper spiritual meaning, she uses these images in her poetry to convey creation's hidden meaning.

---

35. O'Connor, *Mystery and Manners*, 99.

36. Rossetti, *Complete Poems*, 558–59.

37. Westerholm, "In Defense of Verses," 194.

Her understanding of the analogical connection between the physical and the spiritual lies at the heart of Rossetti's symbolic mode of writing. She employs symbols as emblems of Christ's presence in the world. For Rossetti, nature acts symbolically, offering emblems that are imbued by God with special meaning.

CONCLUSION

Creation is made to perform a vital earthly function—by acting as it is intended, these forms symbolically reflect the character of the Maker. This concept stems from the sacramental importance of the material, or the literal, as finding its deepest meaning in the spiritual. Henri de Lubac states, "But this mysterious character of the Bible is not affirmed to the detriment of its historical character. The spirit does not wish to harm the letter. It does not wish to 'destroy the text.' If the reality of the visible world is a figure for the invisible world, then the reality of biblical history will also be a figure for the things of salvation and will serve as their 'foundation.' The deeds and gestures of the personages it presents are, in their very reality, full of a mysterious meaning."[38] To say that literal events of the Old Testament have an associated mystical meaning does not imply that the text is meaningless. Rather, mystery points to the suprarational nature of Scripture. There is always more there than can be understood, and once you think you can explain it, you dive back into deeper mystery. There is a "fullness" to the text rather than flatness.

As we see creation embedded with fullness, so ones's artistic creation flows out of such vision. John Riches declares the work of the poet is to emulate the deeper meaning of creation, stating, "It is indeed a delicate balance: it is too easy for the overzealous to press too quickly to the foundation of things; to scorn the sheer glory of nature or the subtle and half perceived drawings of grace. It requires the poet's—or the mystic's—eye sensitive to the extraordinary richness of creation and the cunning grace in history to continue to sustain a vision of the glory of the world as it is."[39] Through Scripture and throughout all creation, God is not just revealing facts but himself. Communicated through analogy, God takes physical objects and reveals deeper mysteries.

---

38. de Lubac, *History and Spirit*, 104–5.

39. Riches, "Balthasar's Sacramental Spirituality," 176.

Since God communicates through symbols, we arrive at these truths poetically. It requires a meditative and engaged knowing. As Anselm of Canterbury wrote, "Taste the goodness of your Redeemer . . . chew his words as honey-comb . . . chew by thinking, suck by understanding, swallow by loving and rejoicing. Rejoice in shewing, be glad in sucking, delight in swallowing."[40] On these words, David Brown reflects, "Only by such lingering delight over words will their full richness be discovered."[41] The creation deserves this meditative and engaged knowing. It happens by loving the Redeemer, and through the Redeemer, the world that he is redeeming.

In the same way, artistic creation is rooted in deep, engaged, meditative seeing. We must see these created realities through to the Creator behind them. God is the great revealer, and as artists, we have the privilege to partner with God in this revelation.

40. Anselm, "Meditation on Human Redemption," 137.
41. Brown and Loades, eds., "Introduction," 19.

6

Are You Ready to See?
Mystery and Reserve

It is not the subject matter that counts in a painting but the spirited vision at work in it; it is not lovely Beauty that defines artistic quality but a crafted allusivity.

—Calvin Seerveld, *Bearing Fresh Olive Branches*

This prime epiphany of "God who is Mystery" is both an encouragement and a challenge to Christians, also at the level of artistic creativity. From it has come a flowering of beauty which has drawn its sap precisely from the mystery of the Incarnation. In becoming man, the Son of God has introduced into human history all the evangelical wealth of the true and the good, and with this he has also unveiled a new dimension of beauty, of which the Gospel message is filled to the brim.

—Pope John Paul II, "Letter to Artists"

Art has its most profound impact when it invites interaction as people stop to listen, look more intently, engage with new ideas, or see familiar images in new ways. Art inspires us most when we remain with it, and as it remains with us. We learn to see and to feel when we are drawn into the contemplation of an image. This typically happens when we sense that there is more to know or understand than what is seen at first—this very notion compels us to think, to take the time to seek the deeper meaning. This sort of inspiration requires mystery—space between what is seen on the surface and the meaning found throughout the layers of an image.

The Pre-Raphaelite artist William Holman Hunt wanted his art to prompt a meditative response. George Landow states, "He wanted to make the spectator carefully consider the smallest points of interest in his canvases."[1] While Holman Hunt embraced a realistic style, he did not want to suggest that what could be seen at first glance was all there was to see. Instead, the realistic imagery acted as a window into something more, oftentimes, something that could not be clearly seen or adequately represented.

Augustine famously said, "We are speaking of God; what marvel, if you do not comprehend? For if you comprehend, He is not God."[2] God is always beyond our intellectual grasp and reach. In a similar way, there's always something "more" to great art. Great art invites us to *return*—to come and see something new each time you look—and to *contemplate*—to enter more deeply into the work. In other words, there's a certain allusiveness to artistic quality in spiritual works. To riff off Augustine, if you say you "get" a great work of art or can exhaustively explain it, it is not the art you "get." You can't "get" beauty.

The writings attributed to Dionysius speak extensively about the power of beauty to attract us to God. It is the sacramental unity of beauty that allows creation to partake in the life of God, and in turn, to reflect that beauty as an attribute of God. Dionysius assigns names for God, all of which are reflective of God's divine attributes. Beauty is one of those names, a name that carries visual, or aesthetic, connotations. By naming God "Beauty," he presents beauty not as something that represents God but as somehow the foundation and paradigm of all beauty.

Dionysius suggests that God is revealed through creation in symbolic imagery, or types that display a sacramental cohesiveness. His sacramental understanding of creation is illustrated by Thomas Sammon, as he describes the link between "ineffable divine essence and actual, concrete entities."[3] Beauty became a strategy that Dionysius used in order to point the Greeks to the perceived echoes of God in creation.[4] He adopted the imaginative way that Scripture communicates, believing that by embracing beauty they would ultimately be drawn back to the source of all that is beautiful.

God communicates himself to us through our senses, therefore, and beauty can be seen as a primary type, or imprint, that pushes us through

---

1. Landow, *William Holman Hunt and Typological Symbolism*, 16.
2. Augustine, "Sermon 67 on the New Testament."
3. Sammon, *God Who Is Beauty*, 96.
4. Sammon, *God Who Is Beauty*, 128.

itself to see God. Irish poet John O'Donohue writes, "Without the senses, we could never know beauty."[5] If types reveal God, then it is beauty that most effectively allures us to truth and goodness. St. Augustine writes in his *Confessions* that beauty "allures and unites us to the things we love."[6] He describes beauty as a type, claiming it to be a necessary means of attracting us to that which we love; without it there would be no means of drawing us in. Beauty doesn't require an explanation, though it sometimes invites curiosity or anticipation. Beauty might be seen as an instrument, or vehicle, of transcendent realities, used to draw us into union with the One who is beautiful.

THE ALLUSIVENESS AND ALLURE OF BEAUTY

In *The Divine Names*, Dionysius writes more specifically concerning the intended function of beauty. He writes, "[Beauty] thereby draws sacred minds upward to its permitted contemplation, to participation and to the state of becoming like it."[7] Sammon explains, "Consequently beauty provokes the will toward that which the will may not know, or at least may not fully know, it wills. Everything that was, that is and that will be is swathed in the divine being. As the good, God is that which all things desire."[8] Beauty has a sort of magnetic effect, drawing us back to who we are in Christ, as he is the One who is Beauty.

Andrew Louth refers to beauty as the call of the divine, the manner in which God calls us back to himself.[9] He reminds us that the Greek word for beauty, *kallos*, is derived from the word *kalein*, meaning to call. God calls out to us through beauty, and in doing so, calls us back to union with him. Beauty is an invitation into the life of God that is often experienced in mystical encounter. Therefore, beauty remains a foretaste, a shadow of reality, only a glimpse of the fullness of God. In his "Letter to Artists," Pope John Paul II states, "Beauty is a key to the mystery and a call to transcendence. It is an invitation to savour life and to dream of the future. That is why the beauty of created things can never fully satisfy. It stirs that hidden nostalgia for God which a lover of beauty like Saint Augustine could express in

5. O'Donohue, *Invisible Embrace of Beauty*, 40.

6. Augustine, *Confessions*, IV.xiii.20.

7. Dionysius, "Divine Names," 50.

8. Sammon, *God Who Is Beauty*, 133.

9. Louth, "Beauty Will Save the World," 70.

incomparable terms: "Late have I loved you, beauty so old and so new: late have I loved you!"[10] Further, Dionysius writes in *The Divine Names*, "But as for now, what happens is this. We use whatever appropriate symbols we can for the things of God. With these analogies we are raised upward toward the truth of the mind's vision, a truth which is simple and one. We leave behind us all our own notions of the divine."[11] Beauty carries with it a function, and that function is to declare its source. Dionysius believes this to be God's way of alluring us to himself. He points to beauty and uses it as an analogy that speaks of God—it is not a disembodied metaphor, instead, it is beautiful because it participates in the life of God.

Holman Hunt realized that one of the dangers of promoting artistic realism is that it might suggest that we should only attempt to copy creation as it appears, and in doing so project it as a lifeless form. Hunt was concerned that the world as it was represented in realism could potentially be seen as disenchanted, one that he says only represents facts. He was worried that, "a realistic style would create an art that was materialistic, empty, literal, and dead, an art that would destroy imagination in artist and audience alike."[12] Beauty, and all creation alike, never speaks of itself.

Beauty can easily lead us toward idolatry by directing the eye to an object's outer appearance, leaving us to gaze in awe and wonder at its own reflection. This can be true for our vision of such things, but also in our emotion, or memories. C. S. Lewis warns of this, saying:

> The books or the music in which we thought the beauty was located will betray us if we trust to them; it was not in them, it only came through them, and what came through them was longing. These things—the beauty, the memory of our own past—are good images of what we really desire; but if they are mistaken for the thing itself; they turn into dumb idols, breaking the hearts of their worshippers. For they are not the thing itself; they are only the scent of a flower we have not found, the echo of a tune we have not heard, news from a country we have never yet visited.[13]

Our understanding of beauty is often bound not to the reality of the thing itself, but rather to an illusion of it. This is dangerous, as it implies, as Lewis puts it, that we can be taken by the scent of a flower and never truly

---

10. John Paul II, "Letter to Artists," 26.

11. Dionysius, "Divine Names," 53.

12. Landow, *William Holman Hunt and Typological Symbolism*, 16.

13. Lewis, *Weight of Glory*, 30–31.

be taken by the flower itself. This is problematic in that when God creates something beautiful to radiate his glory, we worship the thing intended to illuminate him, rather than God himself.

MYSTERY, HIDDENNESS, AND RESERVE

Christian artists tend to be wary of the notion that in order to be faithful their art must have an overtly spiritual character. However, Christ shows us that reserving certain truths can be just as faithful of an expression. This is not to suggest that we should withhold the good news of Jesus but that we should consider the relationship between the medium and the message. When something is reserved, it is typically being held for future use; it speaks to the benefit of something finding a greater meaning as it is understood over time. While indulging an immediate desire can meet a momentary need in ourselves or others, indulgence is more likely to leave us longing for more, or looking elsewhere for meaning. When the message is "on the nose," Christian art runs the risk of satisfying observers in a superficial sense and losing the opportunity to have a lasting impression.

Divine meaning is oftentimes veiled in creation or within the circumstances of our lives, requiring us to draw it out—to seek and discern what these images say about God. Hiddenness is considered by theologians to be central to God's way of communicating his presence in the world—it is near, yet oftentimes experienced in subtle ways. For instance, the creative work of God in nature doesn't always offer us clear, one-for-one parallels between heaven and earth, though it does reveal something of the Maker. The ordinary, everyday image, a tree or a person, bears some mark of the Creator. While these things act as emblems of the divine, they are not labeled, or found exclusively in places that are set apart as sacred spaces. Many of the artists we point to in this book have exemplified the way in which art can, and perhaps should, replicate God's manner of revealing meaning, which is not always obvious at first glance. David J. P. Hooker mentioned that in his reflection earlier. Sometimes, maybe most times, it is through the process of creation that the divine presence or hand becomes known. The modes taken by these artists to communicate come as a result of seeing the ordinary as sacred, which factors into an artistic practice that demonstrates a hidden quality.

Mystery provides space for an image to reveal gradually, to unfold over time, to develop in the creative practice. When meaning is somewhat veiled, we might even return for a second glimpse and discover something new. Meaning often takes time to come into focus, and is embedded more deeply within our souls when it is slowly digested. For this reason, art should capture our attention and make us desire to know more, to ask questions of the work, and on occasion conclude that we may never know all that there is to learn from an image. By using restraint, artists allow the potential for meaning to take root within the viewer in ways that overt, oversimplistic interpretations may not. We are not hiding meaning but allowing images to reveal meaning as the observer is drawn into contemplation. This concealing is not to suggest that artists should embed hidden codes for the viewer to unlock. Rather, we should appreciate the value of engagement, or coming to know something by experience rather than by a clearly defined explanation. As one sits with a piece of art, participation leads to greater realization. As Mako Fujimura explains in his foreword to Esther Lightcap Meek's *Doorway to Artistry*, "Enduring art tends to hide itself for a while before the viewer begins to understand its true impact."[14]

In many ways, art's hiddenness and mystery is similar to the concept of reserve as developed by Isaac Williams in the Oxford Movement. Reserve is a nineteenth-century concept that resembled the ancient practice of the church to withhold certain doctrine until converts had developed a spiritual imagination to perceive sacred truths. They were concerned about the dangers that could come from the frustration of using intellect alone to understand the things of God. They patiently awaited God to develop an imagination in the believer to understand how to approach biblical truth as Scripture, rather than as explanations for historical or scientific questions.

Williams supported reviving what appeared to be a stagnant church, but he had a growing concern about the particular way the church was going about making converts. The movement that he was a part of addressed a rationalism that lingered from the Enlightenment—when scientific answers were demanded to satisfy intellectual curiosity. In some cases, the church sought to provide explanations in order to make believers, but the rational explanations left no need for faith. Those in the Oxford Movement were concerned that the church was headed down the same path—and urged the church to resist the temptation to reduce God to our ability to explain him.

Williams expressed discontent with some of the trends taking place in English worship gatherings. He was concerned that some aspects reflected the church's desire to explain people into belief. Sermons were often

14. Fujimura, "Foreword," ix.

lengthened and Holy Communion was an afterthought. To Williams, these shifts indicated a lack of credence given to the role of symbolic participation, in lieu of a heightened belief that God can be understood if proper explanations were given. The Word had been held together with the enactment of it through participation in the sacraments. For him, this suggested a reliance on one way of knowing and experiencing God and perhaps pointed to a declining regard for the way God appeals to our imagination for the formation of our souls. Worship became disembodied or excarnated.

Williams, among other leaders in the Oxford Movement, believed that an overdependence on the intellect squeezed out room for mystery and reverence. They had settled for methods of communication that suggested that we can explain or even fully imagine the magnitude of God's character. The appeal to our imagination by way of symbolic participation, including the intellect, was thought to align more accurately with the way God has made us to experience and to understand transcendent, unexplainable, and unimaginable concepts. Symbolism leaves room for mystery and helps preserve a reverential posture toward God.

ARTISTIC RESERVE IN THE PRE-RAPHAELITES

These ideas from Williams, and the Oxford Movement in general, influenced many artists living in his era. Some of those associated with the Victorian movement called the Pre-Raphaelite Brotherhood recognized the way transcendence is reserved, or hidden by ordinary forms. They were set on depicting ordinary, everyday life in a way their predecessors were not. For this reason, their work was often considered to be scandalous, especially when they portrayed religious figures as normal people going about their everyday activities. They were reacting to the over-spiritualist posture of a previous generation—an approach they considered to be unrealistic and disassociated from real, everyday life. The Pre-Raphaelites did not respond with a purely materialist style, but instead sought to capture familiar images with layers of meaning. For many of them, painting stemmed from their interpretation of the world. While literal interpretations could be seen as copies, or imitations of life, much of their work conveyed a deeper meaning that was hidden within real life.

These Pre-Raphaelites offer an example of the way art can act as a curtain that is adjusted to accommodate the state of the observer. By using everyday images in symbolic ways, rather than overt representations, observers can draw a variety of interpretations based on their desire and capacity to see. Interpreting a painting requires more than the ability to accurately peg the artist's intention; seeing requires the observer to have spiritual eyes in order to perceive meaning, which is something that usually develops over time. This manner of interpretation illustrates the way meaning is communicated, not by starting a composition with a particular idea in mind, but instead by expressing a world that is already charged with meaning, which then invites a variety of interpretations based on the eyes of the observer.

GRADUAL REVELATION

As an example of reserve, consider the role of stories. Stories are often used to clarify a point or to simplify a complicated idea. However, Jesus tells stories that are often cryptic, used to conceal or hide important truths. In Mark 4, Jesus concluded the parable of the sower by stating, "He who has ears to hear, let him hear" (v. 9). As the crowd began to recognize that there must be more to the story, they asked Jesus for an explanation. He provided enough understanding for many in the crowd to want to know more. They could not ignore the image and wanted to explore the levels of meaning they sensed were hidden within. He responded, "To you has been given the secret of the kingdom of God, but for those outside everything is in parables, so that they may indeed see but not perceive" (v. 11). This statement implies that this story was meant to veil something from those outside, while understanding was given to those who were prepared to hear. This collection of parables in Mark 4 ends with this statement, "He did not speak to them without a parable, but privately to his own disciples he explained everything" (v. 34). The analogy of a seed is used by Jesus to reveal truths about the kingdom of God. However, this analogy also acts as a veil that conceals these realities from those who were unable to perceive them.

This example often leads people to criticize Jesus for excluding those on the "outside." However, it could be regarded as an act of mercy toward those without understanding, providing time to contemplate these truths, and fostering spiritual health in ways that explanations are unable to accomplish. Similarly, instead of interpretation or explanation, art can be seen as a spiritual seed that God develops over time through the ongoing contemplation of an image.

Symbols allow for the slow release of information, the unveiling of mysteries. Flannery O'Connor states, "Fiction is presented in such a way that the reader has the sense that it is unfolding around him."[15] This way of writing resists the notion of presenting the reader with information that leads to an intended outcome. Instead, it feels more like sitting alongside the writer as you consider an idea together. Visual artists can accomplish this by using real-life circumstances to allow meaning to unfurl over time. The literal is a necessary means through which the reader can take hold of infinite truths. Pictures are necessary instruments that reveal in ways that go beyond wordy description. Artists explore an idea that cannot be told in any other way; a literal symbol is necessary to convey information that has no clear explanation.

George MacDonald speaks to the limitations of words, while still suggesting that words carry out a variety of essential functions. He states, "[Words] can convey a scientific fact, or throw a shadow of her child's dream on the heart of a mother."[16] He proceeds to suggest that just because certain aspects of life are beyond definition, we should not believe words to have no meaning. Instead, he explains, "The cause of a child's tears may be altogether undefinable: has the mother therefore no antidote for his vague misery? That may be strong in color which has no evident outline. A fairytale, a sonata, a gathering storm, a limitless night, seizes you and sweeps you away: do you begin at once to wrestle with it and ask whence its power over you, whither it is carrying you?"[17] MacDonald compares this way of using words to a sonata, a piece of music that imparts truth by enveloping the listener into feeling and experiencing something transcendent. The music isn't written to define a complicated truth—lyrics are not even involved! He invites us to consider the significance of this way of communicating, asking, "Is she therefore a failure, because she is not definite? Is it nothing that she rouses something deeper than the understanding—the power that underlies thoughts?"[18]

15. O'Connor, *Mystery and Manners*, 73.

16. MacDonald, *Complete Fairy Tales*, 8.

17. MacDonald, *Complete Fairy Tales*, 8.

18. MacDonald, *Gifts of the Child Christ*, 27.

ARTISTIC EXAMPLE: DUNCAN SIMCOE

For an example of reserve and the use of mystery, consider the contemporary artist Duncan Simcoe. Simcoe is a practicing artist and art professor at California Baptist University. Traditionally trained in easel painting, he discovered the medium of tar paper in midlife. His ongoing work is called "Black Drawings" due to the black tar paper that he uses and the mystical sensibilities infused in the darkness.[19]

Image Journal recently did a profile of "Black Drawings." Both luminous and foreboding, these line drawings with oil paint and brushes flip the normal contrast. Usually, artists work with a light surface which they enhance through color. But Simcoe starts in darkness and the light emerges through his line and brush marks. This process allows a realm of mystery to be latent within his displayed subjects. On his artist page, he has two quotes: one from the Bible and one from the psychiatrist and literary scholar Ian McGilchrist. He has the Fifty-Forth Psalm: "If I say to the darkness: 'fall on me', and to the night: 'Hide me', even the darkness is not dark to Thee, for the night shines as the day." From McGilchrist, he quotes, "The world is not a brute fact, but like a myth or metaphor; semi-transparent." Simcoe takes the transparency of the world shot through with divine presence and meaning. He has drew reflections on plane crashes and racial tensions and layered them with a sense of mysterious otherness and transcendence.

One such example is a series of works he calls "Mythinburbia." Commenting on the "immense secularity" of suburbia, he displays Southern California postwar ranch-style homes splattered with divine and iconic images. Gordon Fuglie aptly describes two works in a series in *Image Journal*.

> Hugging the bottom of the picture plane, Mythinburbia #10 (Mister Vortex) portrays the stark horizontality of a residential street in a colorless, diagrammatic fashion. In an alarming contrast, a wide, spiraling vortex intrudes from above, recalling the gargantuan disc-shaped spaceships from the 1996 film *Independence Day*. Playing upon the disparity of the mundane and cosmic (or spiritual) throughout the Mythinburbia series, Simcoe intervenes with what he calls "mystical punctuations." As our gaze drops from the ovoid maw of the vortex, we note that the picture window of the house below is filled with a bright green rectangle framing the head of a child who stares out imploringly. Typically, tract houses are set back from streets and sidewalks by needless lawns; there are

19. See some of these works on his personal website, duncansimcoeart.com.

no porches on which to take one's leisure or greet neighbors and passersby. Suburban dwellers are literally sheathed in quotidian isolation—even as eternity descends.

Simcoe took up the notion of suburbia as a desert in Mythinburbia #13 (Rain in the Desert). Using a straightedge, he meticulously drew a residential street view that hearkens more to the abstract precision of a blueprint than a place where people experience joys and sorrows. In the foremost house, he has placed a very wide picture window onto the (perhaps ironically named) living room. Therein we see an actual desert landscape—gray, flat, and sparsely dotted with Joshua trees. Upon closer view, we notice that the desert sky is filled with storm clouds; desolate wastelands eventually do get some rain. Does the picture-window image prophesy life-giving showers for Simcoe's arid suburbia? At the upper left, roiling globby clouds intrude to unleash a messy downpour—metaphorically vivifying much more than the neighborhood's lawns.[20]

Though we're sure Simcoe wouldn't say he's using "reserve" in this series, one can ascertain a level of mystery, hiddenness, and transcendence within the ordinary—things like suburban, cookie-cutter houses. Suburbia can be a site for iconography. The darkness glimmers with radiance.

CONCLUSION

We can certainly learn from the challenges that our ancestors faced and can receive principles that are useful for our growth as artists and as instruments used by God for the sake of the world. Again, this growth requires spiritual sight, an imagination that allows us to see the things of God in the everyday. But, this way of seeing leads us toward a more symbolic representation in art. In the same way that God uses symbolic ways to communicate truths that are beyond comprehension, we should not presume to be able to appropriately define such sacred realities without the use of analogy. For this reason, just like poets, the symbols that have been given to us in our experience of the world are used to communicate unseen realities. By adopting a subtle way of representation, observers are drawn into contemplation, and a variety of senses are touched, allowing these divine mysteries to seep into our being.

20. Fuglie, "Fade to Black."

Artist Reflections—Gary Ball

I LOVE TO DRAW. I enjoy the simplicity of following the contours of a form, the angles and intersections. In the early years of drawing, accuracy was always my goal: how well could I imitate what I was seeing? My first canvases were tithe envelopes from the pew back that I ripped open to draw on. The church service was more influential in my artistic formation than any art class. Over the years of church drawing, my priorities shifted from achieving proper lines and creating depth from shading, to capturing the emotions behind the static images on the page. I can remember illustrating the vague biblical images that I heard my father talking about from the pulpit, and on many occasions, he became the subject of my early drawings. It took years to feel like I could reflect, with any accuracy, extended arms and hands that communicated so much emotion—the passion expressed in clenched fists, or the invitation extended by outstretched hands. These postures conveyed a depth of feeling that I intended to capture on paper. While I gained confidence from the congratulations after a good drawing, it took years for me to understand art as more than imitation.

The simplicity of pencil drawing will always be my first love, but color became more necessary as I began to observe the complexities of life, which led to my desire to take a more meaningful approach to art. Color beautifies and communicates in ways that the simple definition given by lines cannot always achieve. Colors are often associated with various emotions and indicate certain moods—think fiery reds or melancholy blues. In Christian tradition, color conveys symbolic meaning, too—most prominently, blue represents the heavenly realm and red represents the sacrifices or desires associated with our earthly lives. The beauty of particular combinations of colors can fix our attention, and even evoke memories, or make associations with images from nature.

FIGURE 4

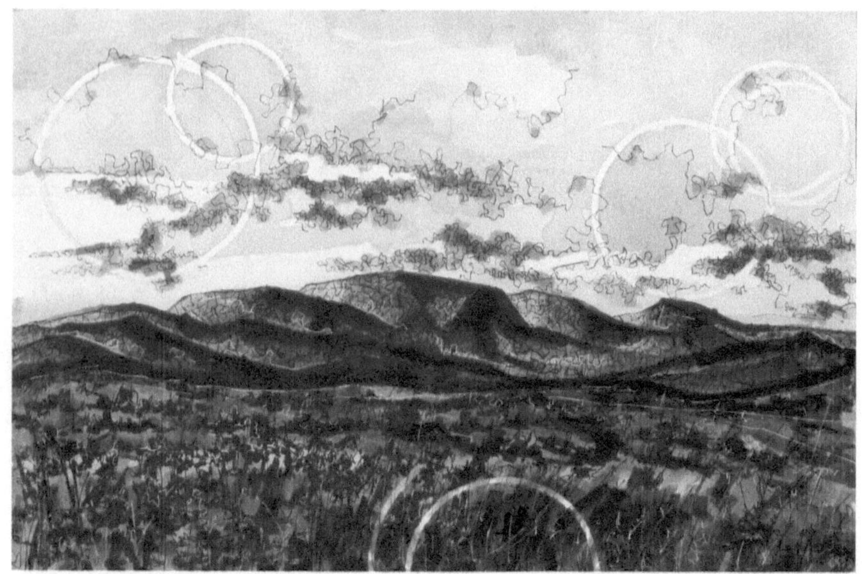

The COVID quarantine provided me with the time to create—or more accurately, the *need* to create. The need to express the depth of emotion and somehow point to meaning beyond physical health was unavoidable. Art became a prayer exercise and a means of contemplation. But practically, I couldn't hole up in my studio, away from my family, and conversely, I didn't want to leave unfinished oil or acrylic paintings on the kitchen table until I could revisit the composition. For these reasons, I took up painting with watercolor—to finish compositions more quickly, and because it is far more tidy than painting with oil. However, while it can be finished more quickly and is easier to clean up, it introduced me to a variety of new challenges.

As a perfectionist, I found watercolor to be an especially challenging medium. It is runny and not as easily controlled as other modes of painting. Details can be more difficult to achieve than if I were drawing, or even painting with oil or acrylic. Watercolor requires artists to practice restraint—I am tempted to overwork a watercolor painting because of my desire to reflect an image accurately. However, the "mistakes" often produce the most beautiful elements of the painting. I am consistently surprised by the color combinations that come from unintentional blending and the way the world inside the lines mixes with that which lies outside. The product is often beautiful and thought-provoking.

Watercolor often runs outside of the intended boundaries. The bleeding of colors can act as a symbol of the sacramental overlap, indicating a participation in a world beyond the material. While I am naturally inclined to arrange colors in an orderly manner, I appreciate the way bleeding color invites one to contemplate the way an image participates in an unseen spiritual reality. This symbolic element wasn't something I intended, rather it is an aspect of watercolor painting that I have come to appreciate. The blending of worlds speaks to me and has revealed a meaningful level that I never expected. This sort of revelation has sharpened my eye, causing me to look carefully for ways that a painting might speak beyond my own thoughts or intentions.

FIGURE 5

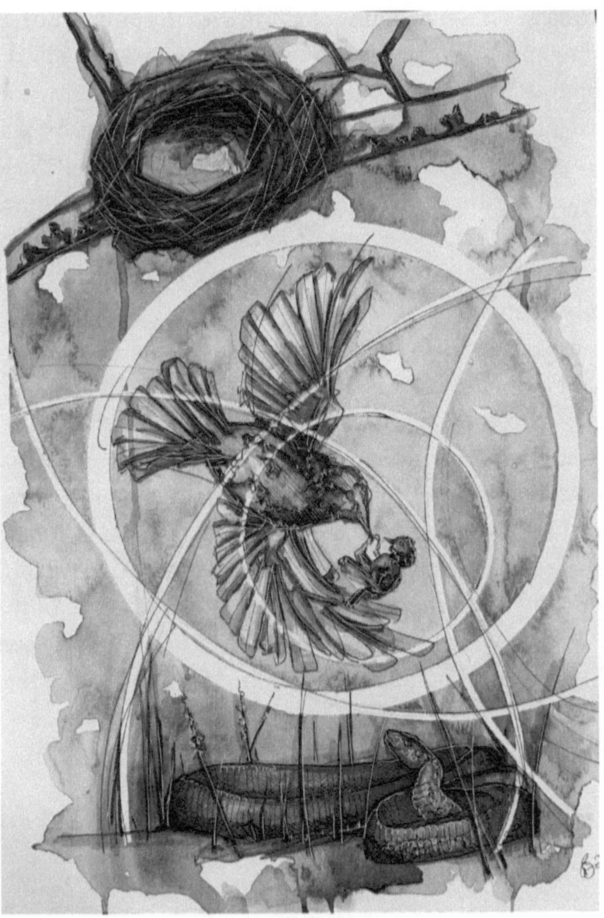

While the unpredictability of watercolor is maddening at times, it has renewed an anticipation within me to discover what a painting will become. Even when I attempt to formulate a plan, each painting still tends to take on a life of its own. To a degree, it is as if I am following the painting's lead, balancing the need to shape and form an image, while resisting the temptation to over-define it. This requires me to be content with mystery, and hopefully, adds a level of interest to those who interact with the painting. I've learned to look more closely, to see what might emerge, as opposed to always projecting ideas or images onto the canvas.

Despite growing more comfortable with less detailed painting, I still combine drawing with watercolor. I typically use ink and marker to give shape to the form and to add dimension. Maybe I'm giving into the temptation to define because I want others to see from my perspective, or to make sure they are clear on the meaning that I intend to communicate. However, I am becoming more accustomed to leaving things slightly undone, and in doing so, inviting others into the work of interpretation. It takes a level of trust to leave interpretation open to each person—to not force meaning—but this allows every observer to come to their own conclusions, either immediately or over time. Hearing people interpret my work has been one of the greatest gifts that comes as I grow in patience. It is a joy to hear the various ways that God reveals to each person, even when it is not what I had originally intended.

The ambiguity that I've learned to live with on the canvas has been reminiscent of my faith. I have become more aware of the ways God subtly communicates and to appreciate the way he patiently draws us into truth by way of participation. This is the beauty of mystery—we worship a God that cannot be defined, yet loves to come near to us. I've recognized the anticipation that has developed in my approach to art is a product of my approach to life. But, it is also true that through this expectation in art, God has taught me to look more intently at the world. Because of the way God has used art to develop my soul, I hold art more loosely as my own and pray that it might be a vessel of grace used by him for the good of the world.

FIGURE 6

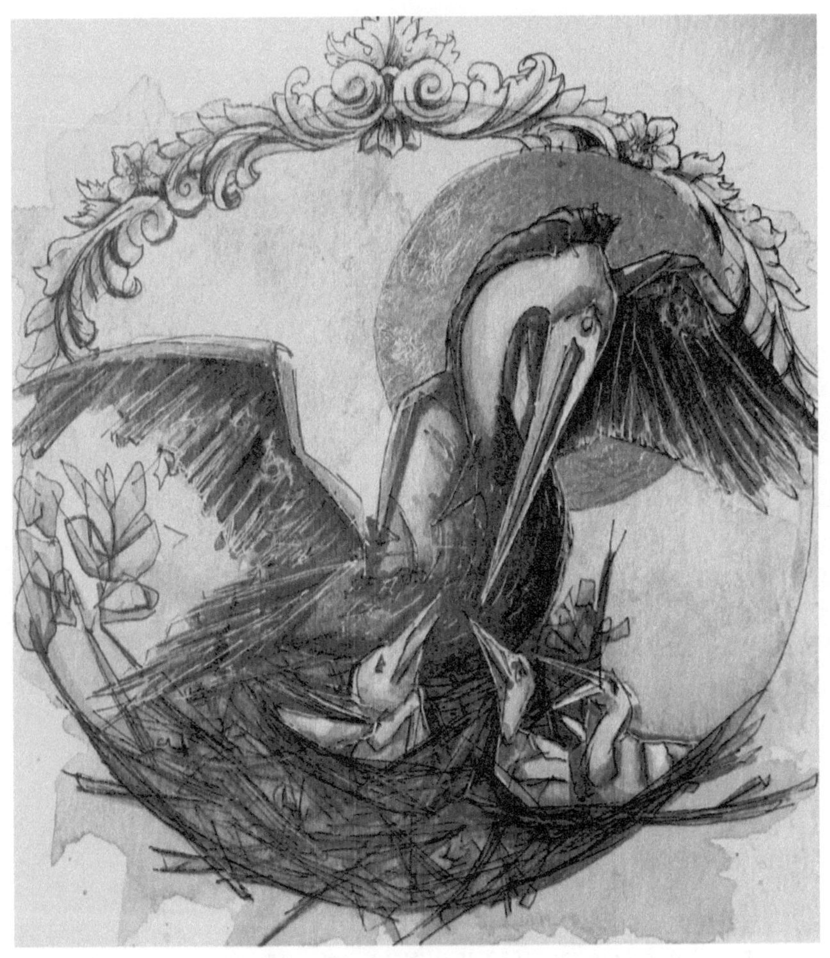

7

Seeing as Participation: Art as Means of Grace

Beauty is what will save us, complete us. This can be found outside us, in nature, or in the grandeur of the cosmos. But in order to open ourselves fully to this, we need to be fully aware of it, and for this we need to articulate it in the languages of art. So created beauty, works of art, are not only important loci of that beauty which can transform us, they are also essential ways of acceding to the beauty which we don't create.

—CHARLES TAYLOR

Art's fruitful womb is the soul's attunement to God.

—HANS URS VON BALTHASAR

THE 2019 FILM *A Hidden Life* was directed by Terrence Malick. The movie features the story of Franz Jägerstätter, an Austrian farmer in a remote village who resisted Nazism and Hitler's demand for absolute obedience during World War II. He refused to fight on the Nazi's behalf. This resistance led to his eventual execution, leaving a widow and three young daughters behind. The title, *A Hidden Life*, is taken from the novel *Middlemarch* by George Eliot, with which the film ends: "For the growing good of the world is partly dependent on unhistoric acts; and that things are not so ill with you and me as they might have been, is half owing to the number who lived faithfully a hidden life, and rest in unvisited tombs."

One of the most powerful moments in the film is when Franz assists a painter who's restoring an aging church. The painter is touching up some fading images, adding plaster where needed, and fixing the outside columns. While inside, the painter says to Franz:

> I help people look up from those pews and dream. They look up and they imagine, that if they lived in Christ's time, they wouldn't have done what the others did. I paint all this suffering but I don't suffer myself . . . What we do, is just create . . . sympathy. We create . . . We create admirers. We don't create followers. Christ's life is a demand. You don't want to be reminded of it. So we don't have to see what happens to the truth. A darker time is coming . . . when men will be more clever. They won't fight the truth, they'll just ignore it. I paint their comfortable Christ, with a halo over his head. How can I show what I haven't lived? Someday I might have the courage to venture, not yet. Someday I'll . . . I'll paint the true Christ.[1]

Painting the true Christ requires more suffering than this fictional painter has undergone. His vision needed refining to paint the suffering Christ.

The *Isenheim* altarpiece by Matthias Grünewald provides us with a vivid image of Christ's suffering. Beauty is sometimes ugly. The cross of Christ is the paradigm of beauty—the alluring power of God whereby God draws us to himself in a way that could never be fully explained or understood. In the midst of despair and anguish, the beauty of the world shines forth. Grünewald's altarpiece depicts the grotesque, the gruesome death and agony of crucifixion, all the while captivating and compelling us in its beauty. Joshua Hren calls this aesthetic "supernatural realism." Art is rooted in the really real but things are also more than they seem.[2] Grünewald, according to Hren, "extracted the very essence of charity and despair from the triumphant depths of squalor and ushered in an art ordained to render the invisible and the intangible."[3] It was a picture of the real that gave more than what it contained.

Grünewald's altarpiece is not only a depiction of suffering, or even intended to reframe the grotesque as something beautiful. This piece was placed in a monastery devoted to caring for patients with skin disease. These patients were invited into a chapel each morning to gaze upon a God

1. Malick, dir., *A Hidden Life.*

2. See also Williams, *Grace and Necessity,* 34–36. The labor of art is a recognition that the "objects of perception were not exhausted by what could be said about them in descriptive, rational and pragmatic terms" (36).

3. Hren, *Contemplative Realism,* 17.

revealed in the crucified Christ, bearing wounds similar to their own. They were lepers, cast out by society, yet invited into the life of God who has made himself present to them through his own suffering. This piece demonstrates the participatory way of knowing that Paul describes in Philippians—knowing God in the power of his resurrection, and sharing in his sufferings, becoming like him in his death (Phil 3:10).

A similar dynamic is at play in the Pietà, where the beauty of God is revealed in the lifeless body of Jesus, held in the arms of his grieving mother. Nancy Bedford states, "In Christ God assumes our suffering, not to glorify suffering in itself but to open the path to abundant life from its true solidarity with the worst things human beings can endure: suffering, torture, death, loss of loved ones."[4] The image of a dead Christ did not appear beautiful by earthly standards but was a bold proclamation of absolute beauty.[5] The crucifixion was always an offense to the senses. Paul proclaimed it to be a stumbling block in 1 Corinthians 2. In this way, cruciform beauty confronts worldly aesthetics, exhibiting that beauty is not always the way things appear, and that absolute beauty pushes beyond the reflection of things as they are.

Suffering is the one aspect of life for which we consistently seek explanations. As we encounter pain we find ourselves wallowing in it, consumed in such a way that it becomes our identity, or we are drawn into the life of God through our identification with Christ's own suffering. He is present to us in our pain, and through it, we come to experience his comfort. Throughout time, artists have captured the emotion of pain better than any other, probably because of their own experience. On the surface, suffering is repulsive. However, in the Christian experience, the hope of the resurrection transfigures our vision of pain, drawing us through it to know, or share, in the life of God. Art takes on an incarnational element when we depict this reality. God is made present to us, particularly in Christ—but to a lesser extent, he is somehow near to us as we gaze upon the wounds depicted by Grünewald or in the grief of a mother that Michelangelo captured in stone.

Of course, one has to be confronted and participate in life with God to see the beauty displayed in the cross. We must be ready to see it. Training requires participation. What role does the artist play in drawing others into

---

4. Bedford, "Beauty of God," 46.
5. Fields, "Beauty of the Ugly," 173–74.

participation? As part of his creation, can we be instruments used to make God present in the world?

PARTICIPATION IN CREATED BEAUTY

In Acts 17, Paul confronts the Athenians at the Areopagus, a gathering place to philosophize and argue. In his well-known speech, Paul alludes to the altar of an "unknown god." Paul doesn't use the familiar tactics of rational argument but argues from the basis of human experience—as if one could reach out and feel God. He contrasts the inanimate gods of the Athenians with the God of heaven and earth, who gives life and breath to all things. Everything finds its being in God, therefore, as we participate in and with creation, we are compelled to seek God and then to find him. Paul seems to indicate that our participation with creation can be an interaction with God and a way to grasp meaning—God is known as we reach out for him. We will know God by seeking him—when we reach out we will discover that he is not far from us. The nearness of God is proclaimed in Jeremiah: "Am I a God at hand, declares the Lord, and not a God far away?" He continues, asking, "Do I not fill heaven and earth?" (Jer 23:23–24). Even in these lofty prophecies, God is both transcendent and intensely personal. The divine Logos has animated creation with his presence, and in doing so, reveals something of his nature.

Christos Yannaras provides a helpful analogy on the accessibility of God in human experience while maintaining what he refers to as the "essential distance that separates us from God."[6] Yannaras suggests, "When we listen to a piece of music by a great composer, Mozart for example, even if we have not heard the piece before we can often identify it as his work. The piece is not simply in the style of Mozart, it is Mozart. In listening to the music we encounter the mind of the composer by participating in his creative act. We have a relationship with Mozart himself, with his personal uniqueness and otherness."[7] Likewise, when we see beauty, we participate in it and grow acquainted with its source. Beauty is communicative and allows us to participate with the divine Maker.

C. S. Lewis also describes a participation with God through creation, stating, "We do not merely want to see beauty, though God knows, even that is bounty enough. We want something else which can hardly be put

6. Russell, *Fellow Workers With God*, 137.

7. Yannaras, *Person and Eros*, 58.

into words—to be united with the beauty we see, to pass into it, to receive it into ourselves, to bathe in it, to become part of it."[8] Lewis explains that our experience of beauty leads us to a real interaction and should not be taken metaphorically—as if saying God is like this beautiful thing. Instead, God is present to us and becomes known through our participation in beauty. However, Lewis warns us that to look upon something and never enter into it is an idolatrous approach that keeps us from experiencing the full essence of the form. Knowing comes through participation.

God graciously reveals himself in the beauty of creation, but he invites us to join ourselves with him by entering into that beauty, especially by participating in his creative activity. We encounter the divine artist in a real and tangible manner through our interaction with the work of his hand. Hans Boersma writes that we participate with God within the "time-bound order of creation."[9] Our relationship with God is not just an "external, or nominal connection."[10] There is a real interaction taking place between creation and God's own life. A rationalist approach to knowing God limits knowing to the information we gather from superficial realities, but sacramental participation introduces us to a way of knowing God that comes from enjoying his presence in the world. Beauty leads to communion.

If it is possible to participate with God by experiencing his activity in the world, we might consider whether it is possible for our art to act as a means of drawing people into participation with God. We have received our being in God, and therefore, we are instruments that find our most significant value when others encounter God in and through our lives. The materials we use—paint, chalk, paper—all come from the hand of God, and therefore, can be the means through which people reach out and find the One by whom all things are created. This participation with God can heighten our sense of fulfillment—by functioning as we are intended, we are used by God for his highest purpose.

The artist has an important role in culture, especially in leading others to discover what might otherwise remain unseen, helping them grasp what had been presumed as unreachable. In Jacques Maritain's *Art and Scholasticism*, he speaks of the role of the artist in a way that is not of this world. He goes on to explain that artists working for beauty are "on the path which leads upright souls to God and manifests to them the invisible things by

8. Lewis, *Weight of Glory*, 42.
9. Boersma, *Heavenly Participation*, 39.
10. Boersma, *Heavenly Participation*, 24.

the visible."[11] Thus, Maritain uses sacramental language: manifesting the invisible things by the visible, alluring souls to God by pointing to the mysterious presence of God in the world.

In Maritain's work, he states, "Christianity does not make art easy."[12] The correspondence between our faith and art emerges out of a well-formed vision. Rowan Williams argues as much when he writes about justice. He suggests, "If justice is a way of seeing before it is a way of acting—the attempt at a response to the environment that is fitting to what the environment actually is—then what is required is an *askesis*, a discipline that keeps us attentive to the ways in which our account of our interests may distort what we see and think we know: an education of the passions."[13] Our passions need education in order for us to see rightly, and part of that vision training is confrontation. Confrontation is a matter of profound significance. Consider your encounters with Jesus that made you reimagine and re-engage the world in which you lived. Often, it is times of suffering, times of confrontation, where we relearn to see. And that resultant seeing is clearer than before.

St. Benedict's first rule in his monastic order is simple: Listen. Art invites us to open our eyes and ears to pay attention, to listen to an art piece, and to discern divine probabilities latent within. The film critic Julia Cameron comments on artistic attention. She writes, "The capacity for delight is the gift of paying attention . . . More than anything else, attention is the act of connection."[14] Art "is born in attention. Its midwife is detail."[15] We do not presume on what God would do but participate in imagining what God could do. Rarely does this imagination work in a linear fashion but the generosity of discovery comes when and where we often least expect it.

As such, contemplation is key not merely for the consumer of art but for the creator. Rowan Williams speaks of listening in this way: "If the stuff of the world can be a medium for communication, the exploration of the possible meanings of what is given becomes a listening for something like a gift, the bestowing on us of a share in a reality that is for our sharing."[16] If Christians are to participate with God, they must learn to draw out meaning

---

11. Maritain, *Art and Scholasticism*, 40.

12. Maritain, *Art and Scholasticism*, 72.

13. Williams, *Looking East in the Winter*, 187.

14. Cameron, *Artist's Way*, 53

15. Cameron, *Artist's Way*, 21.

16. Williams, *Grace and Necessity*, 86.

from creation through contemplation. We might ask: how does this image participate with God simply by being what it is?

Gerard Manley Hopkins demonstrates this way of contemplation in his poem "The Windhover." He describes his vision being "caught" by the sight of a windhover riding upon the wind. The bird is simply doing what it was made to do, a simple thing that draws Hopkins into contemplation. He writes, "Stirred for a bird, —the achieve of; the mastery of the thing!" The mere contemplation of this bird leads the poet to worship God. He isn't stretching to make the bird into a symbol; however, through contemplation, the bird becomes a symbol as it acts according to the divine will. This scene is reminiscent of the words of Paul in Acts, saying, "In him we live and move and have our being'; as even some of your own poets have said, 'For we are indeed his offspring'" (Acts 17:28). These words reflect the animating grace of the Holy Spirit that allows creation to carry out its intended function, and as we participate in and with creation we find ourselves drawn more deeply into the life of God.

Participation is rooted in the belief that all creation is formed out of the Trinity and ultimately functions to draw us back into unity—creation has a vital role in leading us into union with God. We experience a movement toward him as we interact with earthly creation, the goal being that our literal strides are brought in sync with God as we walk with him. Ideally, our participation in the world will lead us toward spiritual alignment with the Creator.

Union with God is a theme that runs through Christina Rossetti's devotional poetry. In "Let Everything that has Breath Praise the Lord," she equates union with harmony, writing, "Tune me, O Lord, into one harmony with Thee, one full responsive vibrant chord; unto thy praise all love and melody, tune me, O Lord."[17] She builds on the idea that God draws us into union by portraying the way nature shares in the Maker's life, simply by being what it is. She longs for the same harmony that is observed in earthly creation. In "When I Was in Trouble I Called Upon the Lord," Rossetti writes, "As rivers seek a sea they cannot fill, but are themselves filled full in its embrace, absorbed, at rest, each river and each rill: Grant us such grace."[18] Rossetti's hope is that by walking according to the will of God, she will gain the same contentment that she perceived in the river as it carried out its intended function. Throughout her poetry, Rossetti's

17. Rossetti, *Complete Poems*, 463.
18. Rossetti, *Complete Poems*, 465.

interpretation of nature exhibits the way participation leads her toward a deeper experience of God. Furthermore, her frequent references to nature are intended to draw readers into a similar participation as they contemplate, with her, the deeper truths that God reveals through his creation.

Rossetti displayed a sense of responsibility to use her craft to draw others to know and love God. Her endeavor to reflect God did not start by improving her craft; instead, it began in her devotional life. She longed to *see* God and to faithfully reflect him in her work. This desired vision is evident in her devotional poetry, which clearly displays her intention to participate with God by leading readers into a deeper understanding of divine mysteries. The desire to reveal religious truths is something that artists often resist, especially as an intentional practice. However, drawing people into contemplation of the divine is not as much a utilitarian impulse as it is a function that flows quite naturally from participation with God in our experience of his creation.

INTENTIONAL ART

Many contemporary artists have an aversion to utility, believing art to be made merely for art's own sake. However, art *is* useful and often facilitates some sort of experience. When our compositions are inspired by our participation with God, they will always convey meaning, meaning that may be more significant than we intend. Our availability to God's purpose is the key, a willingness to be his instrument. Philosopher Hans-Georg Gadamer comments, "The gestures that the artist is able to bring out in his work, the gestures that allow us to interpret our world, are never simply human gestures."[19] Gadamer describes the way an image is both wholly corporeal and wholly spiritual, holding back as much mystery as it reveals. He is critical of separating meaning from an image and considers this isolation as a consequence of vision. Therefore, when artists see the world with the glory of God in mind, their work is never merely a human gesture.

Gadamer explains a distinct shift in the way artists understood their role in society when they began to create communities for themselves. These communities were typically on the periphery of society, isolating them from the greater community. Before this change, artists were interpreting the world alongside neighbors with whom they shared a common understanding, and consequently, their work represented the world as it

19. Gadamer, *Relevance of the Beautiful*, 79.

was collectively perceived. However, the isolation from the community led to the individualization of interpretation and expression. This isolation resulted in observers projecting meaning upon the work, rather than seeking the meaning woven into the image, or taking time to discover the potential hidden significance that might be drawn from their shared experience. Instead of creating art for the edification of a community, art became a reflection of the artist alone—set for mass distribution and consumption because of its visual appeal, rather than its capacity to draw people into participation.

This commentary on art reflects the scientism of the day. As society began to see the world as absent of meaning, or reducible to rational explanations, mystery and wonder were seldom sought or displayed. So, while art continued to be appreciated as the individual perspective of the artist, the artist had no sense of responsibility to the community. This analysis is not to suggest the role of an artist should be to spoon-feed the public, or to make decorations according to the appetites of a focus group, but to consider the capacity of the artist to interpret ordinary events as enchanted, or, at times, to prophetically challenge the norms of society that would lead us toward contemplation and a more thoughtful approach to life. Drawing from William Blake, Malcolm Guite states that the role of the arts is to "awaken the mind's attention to remove the 'film of familiarity,' to 'cleanse the doors of perception.'"[20] Increasingly, though, faith has become a private matter, and therefore, artistic vocation is ever more rooted in self-expression rather than infused with a vision of the world that is held in common.

Faith ought not to be privatized in any aspect of life. Lesslie Newbigin suggests that faith is not actually faith *until* it becomes public. The artist's faith is "published" in their artistic interpretation of the world as "types," creation that is patterned after and points toward Christ. Newbigin writes that when faith is published, we "invite [others'] judgment and—if necessary—correction."[21] Art publicizes the way we see the world, and in so doing, invites interaction, even scrutiny. However, it should bid the observer to stop, to look and/or listen, to resonate, and grapple with its meaning or to discover something new. Balthasar describes the intended function of art as an awakening that happens in the slumbering soul—specifically through a divine awareness.[22] In this regard, art does have a utility (intended or

---

20. Guite, *Lifting the Veil*, 12.
21. Newbigin, *Gospel in a Pluralist Society*, 22.
22. Balthasar, *Glory of the Lord*, 97.

not) to facilitate interaction with the divine Artist. Eric Gill once suggested that all good work is propaganda, it all communicates something. Likewise, Rowan Williams wrote, "Art which is not propaganda is simple aesthetics."[23] This statement is not to say that artists should set out to be propagandists but that a faithful portrayal of any object communicates something of its character, and in the case of typology, it reveals something of Christ, the Archetype.

Rowan Williams refers to making art "as a sharing in the creative labor of God."[24] The utility of creating in collaboration with God is not self-seeking, instead, it is born from the simple desire to see God's will accomplished. This way of creating extends beyond the self-serving art made simply for art's sake and carries a regard for how it will be received. Jacques Maritain distinguishes ways of making art by making the distinction between doing and making. Doing, he says, "consists in the free use, precisely as free of our faculties, or in the exercise of our free will, not with regard to the things themselves or to the works which we produce, but merely with regard to the use which we make of our freedom."[25] This way of creating is completely dependent on appetite without regard to truth. Maritain contrasts *doing* with *making*, suggesting, "Art, which rules Making and not Doing, stands therefore outside the human sphere; it has an end, rules, values, which are not those of man."[26] It's good, right, and necessary to have intention in art, even if that intention evolves or is discovered in the process.

EXEMPLARS OF ARTISTIC PARTICIPATION

There are four artists of varying practices who demonstrate intentionality in their work in a non-propagandistic and pro-contemplative way. They exist in different eras and mediums of art, yet they echo a similar note.

First, the novelist Flannery O'Connor expressed her desire for her art to accomplish God's end, his purpose. She wrote in her prayer journal, "Dear God please help me to be an artist, please let it lead to you."[27] She documented her prayers, asking God to be at the forefront of her consciousness, realizing that any desire may unconsciously seek fulfillment in

23. Williams, *Grace and Necessity*, 49.

24. Williams, *Grace and Necessity*, 48.

25. Maritain, *Art and Scholasticism*, 9.

26. O'Connor, *Prayer Journal*, 29.

27. O'Connor, *Prayer Journal*, 29.

anything but God. Her succinct prayer reveals her intentions, at one point she says, simply, "God must be in all my work."[28] Her journal entries call our attention to her regard for writing as a gift to be used for God's purpose. She writes, "Don't let me ever think, dear God, that I was anything but the instrument for Your story—just like the typewriter was mine."[29]

With this mindset, a Christian will have to work harder than the average artist. Hard work, discerning meaning, and making meaningful art are needed to overcome the modern stigmas associated with Christian art and to reclaim the opportunity to be taken seriously. However, taking our work seriously is a natural consequence of recognizing making art as a vocation, as the apostle Paul urges, "Whatever you do, work heartily, as for the Lord and not for men, knowing that from the Lord you will receive the inheritance as your reward. You are serving the Lord Christ" (Col 3:23–24). Consider that symbolic meaning can help us discern and lead us to new depths in our art-making, and through our effort, lead others to see the world anew. With this participation as our vocation, we will no longer be satisfied with seeing or representing things simply as they appear but aim to reveal mysteries that are discovered beneath the earthly veneer.

Second, the poet Malcolm Guite suggests that Christians should have a depth that may not be achieved without spiritual eyes. We strive to look through material, history, and emotions in an effort to discover a deeper spiritual significance. Guite states, "All great art is a bridge with one foot in the world of comprehension, the visible, the earth, and one in the realm of apprehension, the invisible heaven."[30] To merely reflect surface realities misses the fullness of meaning—it might capture the *what*, but often fails to consider the *why*. To recognize the depth of reality beyond mere reflection demands more of us, especially if we are to faithfully represent it in a song, poem, or painting. Likewise, Balthasar says, "Erudition is, literally the process whereby a person strives to extract or to draw out spiritual and divine life from all the hidden places where it lies concealed. Art's fruitful womb is the soul's attunedness to God."[31] As those attuned to God, we are to discover the spiritual meaning that is sometimes found buried or concealed in hidden places. While this is difficult and might require more, it should add a new depth to the work artists produce. We no longer simply represent

28. O'Connor, *Prayer Journal*, 21.

29. O'Connor, *Prayer Journal*, 21.

30. Guite, *Lifting the Veil*, 21.

31. Balthasar, *Glory of the Lord*, 97.

a human emotion but perhaps dig into the conditions that lead to joy, pain, or suffering.

Third, Victorian painter William Holman Hunt was said to have avoided representing nature for its own sake. George Landow describes Holman Hunt's take on the temptation to merely mirror what artists see or feel—whether it be a sight or an emotion. On Holman Hunt, Landow writes, "He emphasizes 'we were never realists,' for he and Millais—much less Rossetti—were never interested in making 'a representation, elaborate or unelaborated, of a fact in nature' for its own sake, because to do so would destroy the imagination, that 'faculty' which makes man 'like a God.'" Landow continues, "According to Hunt, 'a mere imitator,' who does not make use of his imagination, necessarily 'comes to see nature claylike and finite, as it seems when illness brings a cloud before the eyes.'"[32] Imitation can be significant in that we, as admirers of beauty, and recognizing its source, seek to imitate God's creative action. This isn't a bad urge. However, for Holman Hunt, the danger is that it could express the imprint (e. g., beauty) without actually connecting it back to the archetype. Balthasar says, "God is *there*, but either as an 'unmoved rock in the depths of nature' or fragmented into the many facets of 'mythology,' which is the proper medium of worldly beauty."[33] Imitation as a consistent practice fails to recognize the sacramental union and misses the reason for which forms exist. All of creation exists for a purpose, imprinted by God to point us back to him. So, to merely interpret things as we see them is to neglect the reality of why things have their being.

Lastly, John Ruskin, the Victorian artist and critic, was especially concerned with what he described as understanding the "ends of life" (or the telos) and further observed how our understanding of life influences the way we make art. While he assumed that his audience knew the purpose for which they were created, he claimed that their art revealed they were often uninspired by this purpose. He calls this *apathy*, an unwillingness to proclaim that which we know to be true.[34] Ruskin posits, "Whole areas of mighty history are summed, and the passions of dead myriads are concentrated, in the existence of a noble art."[35] His point is that we have eras defined by the art that was made during a certain period of history. He

32. Landow, *William Holman Hunt and Typological Symbolism*, 19.

33. Balthasar, *Glory the Lord*, 94.

34. Ruskin, *Mystery of Life and Its Arts*, 11.

35. Ruskin, *Mystery of Life and Its Arts*, 28.

was challenging Victorian artists to consider how their art would define their era. Ruskin quite pointedly challenged them to make spiritualized art, warning that if art is not influenced by faith, then we would present a whole swath of history as reductive. By not interpreting our times through spiritual eyes, we are not interpreting our lives as they really are. Artists would then present a depiction that is not true in the fullest sense. For Ruskin, we run the risk of presenting false and reductive reality when we do not reflect the fullness of reality in our art but merely imitate things as they appear.

CONCLUSION

Because spiritual truth is revealed and concealed through the use of analogy, a God-given perception is necessary for discerning these heavenly realities, apart from which the creative activity of an artist is reduced to mere imitation. The depiction of creation in an entirely material way is akin to a rationalist mode of interpretation that denies the existence of heavenly realities beneath and behind the appearance of substance. Conversely, the Tractarians believed that all creation points toward and participates in Christ in various ways and degrees. This teaching inspired many Victorian artists to acknowledge a connected spiritual meaning with earthly creation, the discernment of which requires "ears to hear," or eyes to see where God is made known. Tractarian poet John Keble expresses this sentiment as a prayer: "Give me a heart to find out thee, and read thee everywhere."[36]

To better understand this period of history, the next vignette will highlight the Oxford Movement and its influence on Christina Rossetti.

36. Keble, *Christian Year*, 36.

Pastoral Reflection:
The Pure in Heart Shall See God

If one fails to see the form of Jesus it is not because the objective evidence is insufficient, but because of the guilt of a "darkness" which does not see, recognize, or
receive the Light. . . . Thus, the guilt is not excused by the hiddenness; rather, the
latter becomes the judgment of guilt. The hiddenness is the objective proof that the
guilty have not wanted to see (cf. John 9.39).

—HANS URS VON BALTHASAR

THROUGHOUT THIS BOOK, WE have suggested that learning to see should
be the primary goal of an artist. However, little has been said about how
to obtain this sacramental way of seeing the world. There's a reason for
this absence: there is no formula or method that results in a sacramental
imagination.

However, Scripture does tell us that holiness leads to seeing the Lord.
Hebrews 12:14 states, "Strive for peace with everyone, and for the holiness
without which no one will see the Lord." We are instructed to pursue purity
in order to behold God. A sacramental imagination is cultivated within us,
and ultimately, given by God. But we are told to strive toward holiness in
order to see. There is a participatory aspect of this cultivation. We learn to
recognize the things of God as we cooperate with him. St. Ambrose, writes,
"Only the strong and healthy eyes can see the sun; only the good soul can
see the good. Therefore, let him become good who wishes to see the Lord
and the nature of the good. Let us be like this good and do good works
according to it."[1]

1. St. Ambrose, "Isaac, or the Soul," 64.

"Beholding" implies that we see something of ourselves reflected in the object of our gaze. We become like that image, forming the way we see ourselves and often defining the way we participate in the world. Paul writes in 2 Corinthians 3:18, "And we all, with unveiled face, beholding the glory of the Lord, are being transformed into the same image from one degree of glory to another. For this comes from the Lord who is the Spirit." The implication of this verse is that we become that which we give our attention to—and Paul explains that as we behold the Lord we are being transformed into his likeness. The word "attention" has its roots in Latin, meaning to stretch toward something. There is an active element to learning to see with clarity; to behold something requires us to stretch toward it, and then be transformed by it. We should acknowledge the power of images to transform us, and thus, in our pursuit of holiness, to consider what we are giving our attention to. Participation with Christ allows us to recognize him more readily throughout creation, and in beholding him, we come to see ourselves and the world for what it really is.

In Scripture, sight is often related to understanding—as our minds are illumined, or brought out of darkness, we see Christ more clearly. Clement of Alexandria writes, "How could he not be desirable, who illumined minds buried in darkness, and endowed with a clear vision 'the light-bearing eyes' of the soul."[2] St. Clement celebrates his deliverance from ignorance as a result of Christ lighting his path. His sight had been dimmed, much like Paul, who had scales covering his eyes before regaining his ability to see. Sight refers to clarity or recognition, which implies that there are ways that vision can be clouded. In Mark 10, Bartimaeus, the blind man, asks to "recover" his sight, to be able to see once again. This suggests that he once had sight, but now is blind. In Mark 10:51, Bartimaeas approaches Jesus, who asks, "'What do you want me to do for you?' And the blind man said to him, 'Rabbi, let me recover my sight.'" Jesus responds in verse 52, saying, "Go your way; your faith has made you well." Mark uses a term for healing that could refer to the blind man being made well in a physical or spiritual sense. It is likely that Bartimaeus truly was without sight, in a literal sense, before he was healed. However, his physical healing finds his most significant meaning in that he came out of darkness to behold Christ.

In the Sermon on the Mount, Jesus explicitly relates our ability to see God to the purity of our heart. In Matthew 5:8, Jesus states, "Blessed are the pure in heart, for they shall see God." Sin is bad and "misses the mark."

2. Clement of Alexandria, *Ancient Christian Commentary on Scripture, Mark*, 153.

However, sin can also be an obstacle to sight. While the vision of God was limited for Moses on Mount Sinai, here on the Mount of Beatitudes, we have a clear view of God in Jesus. He comes as the one who is pure in heart, and by our participation with him, we can obtain purity. But there is an ascent associated with it, a mountain to climb as we stretch to see more clearly. As we climb the mountain, our vision is transfigured.

The first step to the cultivation of sight starts with our willingness to ask for it. Just as Bartimaeus acknowledged Jesus as the one who could make him see, we begin our ascent by looking up to the Source. In his conversion, C. S. Lewis recalls his experience of the world being illuminated. It was as if all the material in creation became a reminder of another world. He writes, "That night my imagination was, in a certain sense, baptized."[3] Baptism was not something he did but was something that God did in him. Lewis describes a nearly instantaneous change in the way he saw the world while alluding to the time it took for the rest of himself to follow. Waiting passively for God to change him was not his intention, rather, he recognized that an embodied faith would help lead him to see.

Our dialogue partners in the Oxford Movement had a profound influence on the Victorian poet Christina Rossetti. Their teaching led her to an awareness of the way God gives us the ability to see and led her to consider the ways that sight can be hindered by sin. Rossetti exemplifies the way the pursuit of virtue offers clarity of sight. Participation in the good opens our eyes to see all that is good in the world. We can see the effect that her sacramental imagination has on her art form. Rossetti's desire to see is evident throughout her poetry, as when she writes, "Lord, grant us eyes to see and ears to hear. And souls to love and minds to understand."[4] In her poem "Cried Out With Tears," she says, "Increase our faith that gazing we may see, And seeing love, and loving worship thee."[5] Rossetti relates our perception of Christ with achieving clarity of sight that requires God to increase our faith. In "Judge not according to the Appearance," her prayer is to receive the sacramental vision needed to penetrate what is seen in order to discover what is beyond. Rossetti poetically requests, "Lord, purge our eyes to see . . . Till taught by such, we see Beyond all creatures Thee."[6] In

3. Lewis, *Surprised by Joy*, 181.

4. Rossetti, *Complete Poems*, 392.

5. Rossetti, *Complete Poems*, 393.

6. Rossetti, *Complete Poems*, 418.

this poem, the narrator's eyes need to be cleansed in order to perceive that which is "beyond all creatures" or "within the shroud a butterfly."

Rossetti frequently expresses her desire for union with God, which comes from knowing him as he is revealed in Scripture and creation. Her personal piety is connected to her desire to see God, to discern heavenly truth within the analogies that he has placed in nature to reveal his character. Union with him enables her to perceive the hidden truths in creation, and in a reciprocal manner, the perception of these truths leads her toward union with God.

The Oxford Movement influenced Rossetti by connecting the ability to see, or discern the presence of God, with the pursuit of holiness. John Keble, a primary member of the Oxford Movement, was a poet himself. His work includes common references to *sight* as the sense through which we apprehend the spiritual truths that are hidden within created forms. John Henry Newman speaks of having the *eyes* of faith, and in his sermon entitled "Faith," Edward Pusey refers to faith as the "*eye* of the soul" and explains that "by faith we *see* him who to our eyes of sense is unseen."[7] Pusey continues, "Faith is the eye of the soul, which God has given us, to behold Himself. If we trust the eye of the body in things of earth, much more must we trust the eye of the soul in the things of God. If that which is highest in us, our soul, strengthened and enlightened by God, could deceive us, much more these bodily eyes . . . Faith beholds Him, because it is beheld by Him. It gazes on Him, because He has first caught and fixed its gaze. It sees, because He has given it eyes to see."[8] The Tractarian reference to sight as the faculty through which we discern heavenly realities in Scripture and creation is familiar to Rossetti, and can be read throughout her body of work.

Elsewhere, Pusey continues,

> Our conviction also is of compound character and made up of various emotions: in moral subjects it cannot be mainly intellectual: in Divine things, awe, wonders, the absorbing sense of infinity and of purity, or of holiness, infuse conviction more directly than reasoning: nay, reasoning in that it appeals to one faculty only, and that for a time is erected into a judge, and so, as it were sits superior, constantly goes directly counter to the frame of mind wherein belief is received. The chance sight of a flower illumined by the sun's rays or of the starry heavens, the moon and the stars which God has ordained, impress the feeling of God upon the soul more

7. Pusey, *Parochial Sermons*, 2.2–2.3.
8. Pusey, *Parochial Sermons*, 2.2–2.3.

> than any artificial reasoning from final causes (however clear it
> may in itself seem to be, as in Paley). Like the centurion by the
> Cross we are awed into belief.[9]

Pusey describes "awe" as a sense through which we are led to believe. He wants us to consider the ways, beyond thinking, that God reveals himself to us.

The Oxford Movement leaders believed that personal holiness significantly affects our ability to discern the presence of God through earthly creation. Discernment is not something that is obtained through a particular method; instead, it is given by God as we grow in faithfulness. Seeing God does not result from mere intellectual effort: it is achieved by faith. Pusey provides instruction for how one might grow to perceive spiritual truth, stating, "In religious writings it is plain that the spirit required is a religious spirit; that none can truly understand St. Paul or St. John, whose mind has not been brought into harmony with theirs, has not been elevated and purified by the same spirit with which they were filled."[10] Pusey links growth in knowledge with pursuing holiness in life.

The Tractarians claimed that perceiving heavenly revelation in nature depends on the observer rather than the inherent revelatory value of the object. Newman states, "Inanimate things cannot stir our affections; these are correlative with persons."[11] He expresses the importance of a growing moral sense for the development of our impulse for discerning the voice of God. Newman's statement undergirds the Tractarian belief that distinct individuals are not all capable of discerning God to the same degree; oftentimes, sight remains limited by God. However, among others in the movement, Pusey believed that the capacity to discern God was something that could develop, though developing in such a way remains the work of God. Isaac Williams wrote at length about the purification necessary to discern God's revelation. He claims this sight is given to those who desire a "sensible manifestation of the Divine Presence" and are "desirous to be led on to something better, and require such assistance."[12]

---

9. Pusey, "Lectures on Types and Prophecies," 6.

10. Pusey, *Historical Enquiry into the Probable Causes*, 26–27.

11. Newman, *Essay in Aid of a Grammar of Assent*, 60.

12. Williams, "On Reserve," 1.11.

PURE EYES AND CHRISTIAN HEARTS

In *The Christian Year*, John Keble is clear about the role of nature to impart heavenly truths. In his poem for Septuagesima Sunday, he states how all creation—above, below, within and around us, "Are pages in that book, to show/ How God Himself is found."[13] Keble is equally descriptive concerning the necessity of having eyes to perceive God's revelation in creation below. George Landow speaks of William Holman Hunt's view, stating, "Everything can be an emblem if we can learn to *see* properly."[14] Nature acts as a symbol but the ability to discern that which it signifies requires a particular kind of sight. In his poetry, Keble continues in describing a book that imparts heavenly truths which require "Pure eyes and Christian hearts."[15] The Tractarians frequently warn of the blinding effect of sin, and, conversely, insist that virtue leads us to discern truth with increased clarity. However, despite our efforts to grow in virtue, we are still dependent on God to give us spiritual sight. The ability to see God "everywhere" requires a certain way of knowing that is dependent on moral uprightness. Keble states, "It is easy to perceive, moreover, how precisely the degree of acceptance, which this method of instruction would meet with, would be proportioned to the humbleness and self-denial of the learner, and to his just sense of moral obligation."[16] Pereiro describes Keble's view that the life of virtue, or moral obligation, leads to an instinct for truth.[17] The Tractarians believed that sin blinds us to God's revelation, and therefore, the commitment to a life of virtue should "bring with it a clearer perception of revealed truth."[18]

The attainment of religious truth requires a unique kind of knowledge that depends on moral formation. This Tractarian principle is built on the concept of "phronesis," a practical wisdom that is gained from the desire for and commitment to a life of virtue. Phronesis is derived from Aristotle's teaching concerning moral formation as the key to growth in understanding. The underlying principle is that we cannot receive the means to discern good without first being good.[19] The Oxford Movement expands on the

13. Keble, *Christian Year*, 35–36.

14. Landow, *William Holman Hunt and Typological Symbolism*, 14.

15. Keble, *Christian Year*, 35–36.

16. Keble, "Favor Shown to Implicit Faith," 11.

17. Pereiro, 'Ethos,' 94.

18. Pereiro, 'Ethos,' 96.

19. Pereiro, 'Ethos,' 91.

basic definition of phronesis with a more specific emphasis on orthodoxy and Christian living. The process of growing in spiritual knowledge has a sanctifying effect that influences the way we live. Keble refers to Aristotle's philosophy as a source for developing the Tractarian acceptance of virtue as a precondition for spiritual understanding. Keble states, "This appears to be exhibited in the system of Aristotle, which makes happiness consist in the everlasting contemplating of the highest subject, that can come before the understanding of man; and supposes it to be, most probably, attainable by the discipline of moral virtue."[20]

Joseph Butler, whose writing *The Analogy of Religion* greatly influenced the Oxford Movement, built on the concept of phronesis as a necessary means for discerning truth. Phronesis is a practical wisdom that is obtained by desiring and growing in virtue. This practical wisdom is revealed in our understanding of circumstances and responding appropriately based on a set of values. Aristotle relates this wisdom to "sight" by claiming that a virtuous person "sees the truth in each case, being as it were a standard and measure of them."[21]

Phronesis is a mode of acquiring knowledge that differs from rationalism. The analogical function of nature in communicating heavenly truths requires wisdom that exceeds logic in order to discern the correspondence between spiritual revelation and material forms. We cannot presume to know the One with infinite intelligence; therefore, the conclusions reached through intellectual reasoning alone remain mere hypotheses. The practical wisdom that is necessary to discern sacramental connections between nature and the character of God results from a desire to know God and in seeking to grow in his likeness. Newman explains the influence that desire has on our actions, and further, the way it leads to spiritual understanding, stating, "When men begin all their works with the thought of God, acting for his sake and to fulfill his will, when they ask his blessing on themselves and their life, pray to him for the objects they desire, and see him in the event, whether it be according to their prayers or not, they will find every thing that happens tend to confirm in them the truths about him which live in their imagination, varied and unearthly as those truths may be."[22] Newman's statement implies that the knowledge we ultimately obtain is profoundly influenced by that which we set out to discover. In

20. Keble, "Implicit Faith Recognized by Reason," 26.

21. Kraut, "Aristotle's Ethics."

22. Newman, *Essay in Aid of a Grammar of Assent*, 64.

terms of religious truth, when we are attuned to God's desires, we develop an instinct for where the spiritual realities that permeate creation are to be found. Pereiro speaks of Keble's "firm conviction that the search for truth could not be separated from the pursuit of goodness." He goes on to state that it is impossible "to discern the good to aim at and the means to achieve it—without also being good."[23]

Pusey considered understanding to be a gift from God; therefore, growing in love and character was necessary for receiving spiritual understanding. Pusey emphasizes the need for love. In his sermon entitled "Will Ye Also Go Away?" he states, "Love God, and you will understand of Him all which can be understood in the flesh."[24] This instruction reveals the same practical wisdom displayed throughout Tractarian teaching. In his sermon "Faith," Pusey preaches, "Meditate daily on things of Eternity, and, by the grace of God, do something daily, which thou wouldest wish to have done, when that day cometh . . . heaven is above our heads, yet we see it not with eyes fixed on the earth." He continues, "Do the works of Christ that thy faith may live. Let love give life to thy faith, works prove it."[25]

Keble believed that the degree to which religious truths are understood stands in direct proportion "to the humbleness and self-denial of the learner, and to his just sense of moral obligation."[26] For Keble, moral qualities were preferable to intellectual knowledge when seeking religious truth. He states, "Moral rather than intellectual proficiency, is the appropriate qualification for that noblest of all studies . . . It has become more and more evident, that we must look to the best man, not to the accomplished or most able, for the soundest views on moral and religious subjects."[27] For those who deny divine revelation, human reasoning is the primary faculty used to find truth. However, for those who believe that God reveals truth in ways that exceed our senses, a different way of reason is necessary—a practical wisdom that leads to an instinct for truth. This way of knowing requires virtue to acquire religious knowledge and growing in knowledge deepens faith, promotes holiness, and leads to humility. Isaac Williams, in his tracts on reserve, averred that advanced doctrine should not be preached or taught to those who do not display an awareness of the need

---

23. Pereiro, 'Ethos,' 91.

24. Pusey, *Sermon Preached before the University of Oxford*, 19.

25. Pusey, *Parochial Sermons*, 2.17–2.18.

26. Keble, "Favor Shown to Implicit Faith," 13.

27. Keble, "Implicit Faith Recognized by Reason," 24–25.

for redemption and exemplify it in Christian growth and maturity. This reflects the Tractarian view that religious understanding requires virtue; therefore, moral instruction should always be taught alongside theology. Theological knowledge, or understanding, should lead to moral uprightness. The pure in heart shall see God, so if we want to create beauty that reflects the Beautiful, the best place to start is spiritual formation.

8

What Use Is the Church for Artists?
Together in Community

A COUPLE OF YEARS ago, we attended a panel discussion that involved a variety of Christian artists. It was all well and good for awhile, but then the conversation took a sharp turn after a comment struck a nerve with the moderator. He proceeded to passionately express his ongoing frustration with the church (as any gathering of Christian artists tends to do). He clearly expected the affirmation of those in attendance, and perhaps rightfully so given the church's failure to support artists. The few scattered "amens" and the occasional nods of agreement fanned the flame of his grievances. He listed the common rifts between church and artists—struggles that are often related to feeling misunderstood—the church doesn't get artists, and therefore, doesn't appreciate their art.

We agree with many aspects of this artist's lament. We could all list a variety of examples of the church's underappreciation of the role of art. The bare walls in many of our churches might be an indication of the common disregard for the way people are formed by the space in which they worship and their aesthetic, embodied experience. The lengthening of sermons might also speak to the common preference of explanations over symbolic representations. We see these as valid concerns; however, we're not convinced that the way art is used within the context of the Mass or Communion is our greatest shortcoming. Instead, we think the formation of imagination is the most significant deficiency of the church's involvement with artists.

While we could empathize with the artist's frustration, our most natural inclination was to defend the church. Granted, it is difficult to relate to a church that does not appreciate art. This artist's concerns revealed a discrepancy between how artists see themselves fitting into the life of the church and the value that the church places on the contribution of artists to its life.

Whether fairly or unfairly, our sense was that the artist was asking the church to submit to him—specifically, that he would be able to freely express himself. While there is certainly a place for expression in the church, a level of submission is required for a Christian. When art is seen primarily as an act of self-expression, artists run the risk of inviting commiseration rather than contemplation. While we value the vision of God as seen through the particular lens of an artist, the intention is to be drawn into deeper contemplation of the divine, rather than appreciating a particular artist. Bernini's sculpture of Teresa of Avila comes to mind as a good example. His fingerprints are all over this piece, but we are not drawn into Bernini's plight. Instead, we are drawn into the life of God through Teresa's ecstatic expression.

To be fair, the church has often failed to provide a framework for artistic thought. Consequently, artists are formed by an alternative framework drawn from modern or secular thought (as noted in the first two chapters). For instance, the church might ask artists to compromise in order to make art *function* within the context of the Mass. The act of making it function can be viewed as compromising the very nature of art. Conversely, we've heard it said that the cathedral is the perfect form of art, precisely because of its function. Participation is the principle at work. Participation could refer to the effective use of a building or vessel, or the way observers interact with a piece, drawing out meaning that might lie beneath the surface of an image. Regardless of the context, a sacramental imagination (which the church can help cultivate) provides artists with a spiritual framework that is applicable to art made either for the cathedral or the gallery.

The general confusion that exists between artists and the church hit home in the surveys we mentioned in the introduction of this book. We discovered that artists were genuinely confused about how they are to participate in the church and unaware of the church's contribution to their formation as artists. While they expressed the desire for their faith to influence their outside artistic vocations, 70 percent of them stated that they either *never* or *rarely* incorporate spiritual ideas in their art. We realize as Christians we interpret the world through a spiritual lens, but Gary's research revealed a *purposeful* separation of their faith from their art, as if the two can exist separately. Art made for *outside* observers was described as self-expression while art *inside* the church is for God. Gary's research showed a clear sense that our artists approached secular and sacred art in very different ways, with little to do with each other. A separation is at work—dividing our perception of spiritual and material realities, separating our practice into sacred or secular, and sadly, creating a distinction between our faith and our artistic vocation.

A sacramental vision joins the spiritual and material. The church owes our artists formation more than it owes them opportunities. If artists need a renewed imagination, that imagination has a divine source. And artists cannot participate in Christ without his body. We need one another. The relationship between the church and artists is reciprocal in many ways. While artists need church, through which the Spirit enables them to see, the church needs artists to help us see anew. In the likeness of our Creator, artists use material forms that are sanctified by God to communicate grace in ways that words cannot. Artists have a unique role, used by God, to refocus our vision on that which is true, while healing the eyes of those who have not yet beheld the sight of God.

In what follows, we'll discuss how the church shapes artists and how artists can assist the church in reciprocal ways. First, the church trains the vision of artists while artists can help restore mystery and reverence for the world. Second, the church provides a story and community for the artists, while artists shape space and place. Lastly, the church can be a place of rest and depth for the artists, while artists can express what's there in the depths.

RECIPROCAL EFFECT NUMBER 1: VISION AND IMAGINATION

Church Cultivates Vision

As noted in the previous chapter, the church has a role in the life of all believers to help them learn to see things as they really are. As the church, we gather together on a weekly basis to be reoriented to that which is real—our focus is retrained to see earthly creation as a shadow of heavenly realities. This reframing is the obligation of the church. Through worship we are forming a particular way of seeing the world. We don't set out to train artists but to form their sight.

Stanley Hauerwas speaks of the way our perception influences our way of being in the world, stating, "For we can only act within the world we can see, and we can only see the world rightly by being trained to see."[1] This statement places the development of vision as a fundamental aspect in determining how we interact with the world. A well-formed spiritual perception influences both the way we recognize and express meaning. In *Resident Aliens*, Hauerwas and Will Willimon state that it is the act of worship through which we are *trained to see*. "In worship, we are busy looking in the right direction."[2] Ideally, the spiritual perception formed in the context of worship will enable us to recognize the literal, material forms as portals into deeper, unseen mysteries. A sacramental imagination enables artists to move beyond mere imitation, or the portrayal of things only as they are seen—for, as Lewis puts it, there is no good telling us about a country we already see.[3]

Artists need the church to lay the groundwork from which they produce their work—to form their vision. In her book on the Celtic imagination, Esther De Waal reminds us of the extraordinary amount of poetry that comes from the British Isles. Referring to their inspiration, she states, "They lived in places of extraordinary beauty. They saw the world through eyes washed miraculously clear by continual exercise; they saw with 'rinsed eyes' . . ."[4] When our eyes are left untrained, artists can easily become imitators of superficial realities. In this way, artists, even those of the Christian variety, will likely either take a materialist or spiritualist approach to making—portraying forms as they appear, apart from any deeper meaning, or bypassing the realities of life all together in favor of a future heavenly experience (think Christian radio). A sacramental vision joins the heavenly and material leading artists to draw out meaning hidden beneath the earthly shadows.

Artists Help Recover Mystery

While the church trains vision, artists help provide new ways of seeing mystery and a holy reverence to life. Consider the Oxford Movement that was described during the last vignette. They sought to confront an

1. Hauerwas, *Peaceable Kingdom*, 29.

2. Hauerwas and Willimon, *Resident Aliens*, 95.

3. Lewis, *Great Divorce*, 83–84.

4. De Waal, *Celtic Way of Prayer*, 96.

over-rationalist approach to Scripture. They desired to recover elements of mystery and reverence in God and in creation.

The primary means the Oxford Movement founders used to resist the infiltration of rationalism was the recovery a patristic hermeneutic that was allegorical in nature. Gary was first drawn to this movement as an artist because of the imaginative character of this interpretive approach. It was inspiring. The Oxford Movement put into motion a revival of the arts that may be seen most clearly in the Pre-Raphaelites, a brotherhood of artists known for using ordinary images in symbolic ways. The Oxford Movement also sparked a resurgence in poetry (think: Christina Rossetti and Gerard Manley Hopkins), hymnody, and encouraged the retrieval of Gothic architecture. This revival in the arts was largely born from a movement that emphasized a particular, typological, way of reading Scripture. These artists were influenced by the church, their imaginations ignited, and in turn they put their gifts to use in service of the church—in the Mass and in the gallery.

The rationalist approach attempted to provide adequate explanations for God. And, while rationalism was intended to *lead* people to faith, by the time it finished explaining God, there was no need for faith. John Henry Newman states, "And thus a rationalistic spirit is the antagonist of Faith; for Faith is, in its very nature, the acceptance of what our reason cannot reach, simply and absolutely upon testimony."[5] The rationalist effort to produce belief through scientific explanations, based on material evidence, negated the possibility of a spiritual dimension to creation or Scripture. Emptying earthly substance of spiritual meaning can lead to a disembodied faith that regards God as impersonal and experienced only from a distance.

In response, the church sought to recover mystery and regain reverence for the One who was beyond our ability to conceive through intellectual means alone. Arguments simply aren't enough. An unexpected, but apparently welcome consequence of the Oxford Movement was a renaissance of a variety of ceremonial elements. Artisans were put to work making vestments and tapestries. Churches were planted in the slums, and due to the number of illiterate worshippers, there was an increased reliance upon the imagery in stained glass and even the proper function of the church building's design to narrate the worshipper into the story of our faith.

The contribution of artists to the life of the church was an essential component of the movement. The influence of the church upon Victorian

---

5. Newman, *Essays Critical and Historical,* 30.

artists was evident throughout the culture, the appeal to spiritual realities could be discovered either overtly or in the symbolic portrayal of everyday images. They submitted to the necessary boundaries presented by the ordering of the Mass; however, they carried these principles into the world—their work infused with mystery and reverence for God.

Victorian artist and critic John Ruskin often referred to the connection between earthly and heavenly realities. He was influenced by a typological, or symbolic, reading of the biblical text. For Ruskin, creation is permeated with layers of meaning that can be accessed through a particular way of seeing. He describes this vision, saying, "It never stops at crusts or ashes, or outward images of any kind, it plows them all aside, and plunges into the very central fiery heart." Ruskin explains, "It gets within the fence, cuts down to the root, and drinks the very vital sap that it deals with."[6] While he doesn't label this vision as sacramental, he uses familiar terminology, describing it as an imaginative practice that involves penetrating the outer shell, the literal or material level, in order to consider what it might reveal about the Creator.

He instructed artists to portray the spiritual and material union in their artwork, to communicate "the signature of God upon his works." Ruskin suggests that the Christian vision is tested, and that we can glean more from nature than what it reveals to the common eye. Ruskin states, "I believe that the eye cannot rest on a material form."[7] What Ruskin details here is that it is lazy for artists to not depict the heavenly realities of the world. He contends that it is the job of the artist to interpret creation as imbued with divine meaning.

Sacramental vision led Ruskin and others to a more joined view of the world. The divisions between sacred and secular art were reduced as the vision shaped by the church led worshippers to see all the world as sacred. The increased use of symbolic realism in Victorian art demonstrated the way people began to sense the nearness of God through all reaches of life. This mode revealed a way of seeing, but also served to teach people to see. They didn't accomplish this through overt interpretations, but by means of symbolic representations that required contemplation, for observers to draw out meaning.

6. Ruskin, *Modern Painters II*, 358.
7. Ruskin, *Modern Painters II*, 225.

RECIPROCAL EFFECT NUMBER 2: COMMUNITY AND PLACE

Church as Foundational Story and Community

Along with providing training in vision, the church gives artists a story and a community. The modern world alienates almost every aspect of existence, and the art world can also inculcate the fragmentation that the world encourages: the separation from land, from place, from action, from the physical world, from the church, from others. Rather than embedded in story and community, there can tend to be an ideal of the "tortured individual genius" motif that artists aspire to. The art world is rife with examples of those who are exceptionally gifted, albeit loners, who end up going mad.

But the church tells a different story. If I can riff off Alasdair MacIntyre a bit, "We can only answer the question 'What should I create' if we answer the prior question of 'What story or stories am I a part?'"[8] Morality and creativity are tied together in our collective story. Essential to humanity is a narrative life. The church gives artists a story to find their truest self in the presence of God with the people of God. As Pope Benedict wrote to artists, "Sacred Scripture has thus become a sort of 'immense vocabulary' (Paul Claudel) and 'iconographic atlas' (Marc Chagall), from which both Christian culture and art have drawn."[9] The story—written and represented—has been the catechesis of artists throughout the ages.

If we take Josef Pieper's suggestion that "leisure is the basis of culture,"[10] and culture finds its root in *cultus,* or divine worship, then all of our creative endeavors are founded in the essential story of divine worship. The gathering, forming, worshipping, and sending communion of the church gives artists a true and compelling vision of a world created, fallen, and redeemed. The church creates a kind of people who can create out of their deepest, most authentic selves as redeemed selves rather than the expressionist, individualistic self.

Flannery O'Connor argued that every artist is a regional artist. Communication can only happen inside a community. For O'Connor, "To call yourself a Georgia writer is certainly to declare a limitation, but one which, like all limitation, is a gateway to reality."[11] Or what Jennifer Allen Craft says

---

8. MacIntyre, *After Virtue,* 216.

9. John Paul II, "Letter to Artists."

10. Pieper, *Leisure.*

11. O'Connor, *Mystery and Manners,* 54.

about communal singing can be true of the visual artist as well: "submission actually increases freedom rather than diminishing it, with the expansion of one's own individual sensibilities about the world occurring in communal dialogue."[12] This limitation of the church community is for the sake of others. In a "global world" that seeks life without limits, the church's story celebrates our placedness, not because it limits us, but because the reality is that we all see from a particular place. This placedness does not limit our seeing but helps us see as far as possible. The region from which Christian artists see is the ecclesial community and the story it tells.

Simone Weil is worth quoting at length on rootedness:

> To be rooted is perhaps the most important and least recognized need of the human soul. It is one of the hardest to define. A human being has roots by virtue of his real, active, and natural participation in the life of a community which preserves in living shape certain particular treasures of the past and certain particular expectations for the future. This participation is a natural one, in the sense that it is automatically brought about by place, conditions of birth, professional and social surroundings. Every human being needs to have multiple roots. It is necessary for him to draw wellneigh the whole of his moral, intellectual and spiritual life by way of the environment of which he forms a natural part.[13]

The unchurched artist is as much as a myth as the unchurched Christian or the placeless person. As Wendell Berry has poetically put it in his poem "A Timbered Choir," where he pictures modern society forsaking place in pursuit of the nameless "objective": "I came to the city that nobody recognized because it looked like every other city." But the result of such a pursuit is in the poem's ending: We never knew where we were going because we never knew where we came from.

The result of placelessness is homelessness. And without the church community, artists will end up homeless, which is perhaps why artists feel homeless, or at least "border stalkers."[14] While we want artists to be those who "care about culture" by "border stalking" on the margins, we also want artists to have a home in the church. Otherwise, they'll be catechized by the story that culture tells rather than the story that the church tells.

---

12. Craft, *Placemaking and the Arts*, 211.

13. Weil, *Need for Roots*, 43.

14. Fujimura, *Culture Care*, 58.

If artists are to care about the church and to care about the world, then (to beckon Wendell Berry again), it all turns on affection.[15] It's not what the church can get from artists or what artists can get from the church, but we build each other up by the mutual care of one another. In other words, we need mutual stickers rather than boomers. Boomers are those who pillage and run. They exploit, take what they can, and move on. They are motivated by greed and money and success. Stickers, on the other hand, are motivated by affection and love for place. They love the place they make in the world. They live with a long view in mind, are stable in place, and therefore restore and regenerate their community.

I am reminded of one of my favorite films called *The Last Black Man in San Francisco*. The main character is named Jimmie Fails, and San Francisco has treated him poorly. The movie features none of the "well-known" San Francisco but highlights all the forgotten places. In many ways, it's the tale of macro-gentrification in a micro story.

Towards the end of the film, Jimmie is sitting on a bus. He overhears a conversation of two mobile, white, hip young professionals. They say they hate San Francisco and are contemplating a move to Los Angeles out of this "dead city."

"Excuse me," Jimmie says, "Do you love it? . . . You don't get to hate it unless you love it." Only Jimmie has the authority to criticize his place. He's the one who knows his place well enough to love it in its fullness. He's been forced to pay attention to the whole place: the good and the bad. He's motivated by affection. In the same way, we're not particularly bothered by artists who critique the church. For the most part, we probably agree with their diagnosis. But they need to have affection for it first, and affection requires roots.

Artists Shape Place

"We shape our buildings; thereafter they shape us."

In Jennifer Allen Craft's *Placemaking and the Arts*, she writes, "In a social context, the arts serve to simultaneously place and displace, uprooting old ways of thinking and acting, while re-placing them with new contexts that communicate, hopefully, a vision of the kingdom and the beauty of the

15. Berry, *It All Turns on Affection*.

cross."[16] If the church helps provide a story and community, then an artist can help shape and cultivate that place and story. Artists can help place us and displace us, as they cause us to enter the imagination of another or apply the placed truth to new considerations and contexts. They help us imagine new creation when we grow bored or limited by the creational realities we live with. As Craft suggests elsewhere, "The arts can give form to seeing the world in a whole new way."[17] Artists can portray how the world *ought to be* and not just what a place *is*.

Walter Brueggemann makes a distinction between space and place. He writes, "Place is space that has historical meanings, where some things have happened that are now remembered and that provide continuity and identity across generations. Place is space in which important words have been spoken that have established identity, defined vocation, and envisioned destiny . . . Place is indeed a protest against the unpromising pursuit of space."[18] In such a way, how we imagine and shape place forms and shapes us. Space is formative and not merely decorative.

We think the problem that we've seen over the past fifty years or so of church architecture is its pure pragmatism. If place shapes us, what happens when we design churches after pragmatic and consumeristic shopping malls? And how has our rationalistic reading of Scripture reduced how we think about place? When the church isn't a building but a relationship, then we design our church like no place. In such an imagination, artists can help churches not just decorate spaces but help with the imaginative creativity that comes with making anything. They can point the church beyond modern obsessions with utility and pragmatism. In that way, everybody is an artist just as everybody is a theologian.

Even if one considers the ways that Christians have used art poorly or in kitschy ways in the past hundred years, one can see the catechetical effect. Though Protestant churches often don't have the ornate and beautiful stained glass windows that historically taught illiterate congregations, we had something as simple as the proverbial felt Bible stories. We don't think any of us would say that this sort of beauty elects us and sends us on mission, yet there was a sensory education that this provided people. The lack of catechesis and biblical knowledge of emerging generations is well documented. Perhaps one reason to blame is not just intellectual formation but

16. Craft, *Placemaking and the Arts*, 177.
17. Craft, *Placemaking and the Arts*, 28.
18. Brueggemann, *Land*, 4.

aesthetic formation—picturing the truth to know the story. Our argument is not that maybe we should get felt Bible stories out of storage, but how can artists help churches catechize young and old? How can churches utilize artists to shape and refine taste along with their theological imagination?

Roger Lundin imagines the role of artist to the world and church as one of a prophet, but a prophet that emerges from and belongs within the church—not dropped mysteriously from another realm. He writes, "Instead, they speak as human creatures who have received the truth handed down through the ages and who hold the treasure of the gospel in earthen vessels. We understand ourselves most fully, as artists and as Christians, when we can see our individual dreams, whether spiritual or aesthetic, as parts of a much more comprehensive story that has already begun, the outline of whose ending is known but whose details have not yet been told in full."[19] These realities are one of the reasons why its so important for artists to find themselves as part of the church. They steward the story that is given and received.

RECIPROCAL EFFECT NUMBER 3: WORDLESS DEPTHS

Church as a Place for Depth

Lastly, the church can help artists access the deep parts of themselves and of the world.

A few years ago, I (Alex) sat in a hospital room with my wife as my daughter was treated for a rare heart disease. For six days, she had a fever hovering around 100–105 degrees. In the years of COVID, only one parent could stay the night. With church on Sunday night, my wife stayed in the room, while I took my other two children to church.

"Are you going to church as a 'regular church member' with the boys?" my wife asked.

"Probably," I replied.

"Let all your tears out . . . It's the only place you allow yourself to cry."

Now, Gary is a frequent crier. It's hard to find a day he doesn't shed a tear or two. But me? I bury my feelings deep down and don't let them ever come up. I have hobbies. I work out. I don't cry . . .

Until I get to church.

19. Lundin, "Offspring of an Odd Union," 147.

Perhaps I feel what most of modern society feels: it's not acceptable to cry in public. But maybe the church is one of the last places where you can cry without question or judgment. It's okay to feel deeply—whatever feelings you may bring.

In our work world, there is no time for rest or leisure, and therefore no time for divine worship, which means no time to get to the essence of things. We settle with faux feelings and sentimentality, because it's quick and easy. If we never rest, we never receive. Josef points out that artists and priests are similar because they both "keep alive the remembrance of a face that our intuition just barely perceives behind all immediate and tangible reality—the face of the God-man, bearing the marks of a shameful execution."[20] So, both artists and priests encourage gazing at the real. The church has material objects, like bread and wine, but the material object is never the main point, though it actually takes on more meaning when it's not the main meaning. The intuition behind all immediate reality is what we all long for. The distinct temptation of artists, though, according to Pieper, is that they can be tempted to create out of projection rather than reception.

In a sentimental world full of faux emotion, in the quietude of the church's liturgy, artists and others can finally sit without distraction, noise, or entertainment. We can receive feelings from the depths that have been hidden, worked over, and buried beneath. In so doing, we can receive the essence of things, the truest realities, the compelling face behind all immediate and tangible reality. We can stop running and rest as we allow the deepest parts of reality to bubble up to the surface. As such, Pieper continues, leisure is "a mental and spiritual attitude . . . of non-activity, of inward calm, of silence; it means not being 'busy,' but letting things happen."[21] We can recognize this reality, and we think artists know what Pieper means, where the creative process feels like "letting things happen" out of calm and silence.

And if we can do that in the space of divine worship, then artists can also sit here with us, receiving the real, and then creating from the grace that is given to them. The church can give space for the cultivation of deep artists rather than superficial ones. Creativity is rooted in reception.

Beckoning a sacramental imagination, Pope John Paul II writes in his "Letters to Artists," "Artists are constantly in search of the hidden meaning

20. Pieper, *Only the Lover Sings*, 62.

21. Pieper, *Leisure*, 46.

of things, and their torment is to succeed in expressing the world of the ineffable. How then can we fail to see what a great source of inspiration is offered by that kind of homeland of the soul that is religion? Is it not perhaps within the realm of religion that the most vital personal questions are posed, and answers both concrete and definitive are sought?"[22] Wonder is the work of worship and wonder is the work of an artist.

To Go Where Words Fail

If the church is a place for depth, artists help plumb the depths to bring it out for others. Church allows a space for depth, while artists have the ability to express what's there when we contemplate. People of "book" and people of "images" need one another. As words increasingly fall short, vision rises in importance. The "book" knowledge and "image" knowledge affect the imagination in different ways. They are not in competition or separate spheres of knowing, but two expressions of the ineffable—something akin to cataphatic (word) and apophatic (image) theology.

My (Alex's) story of enchantment is one that starts with artists. The church had the resources but either I failed to see them or I failed to lean into them. I was one who thought art—at least the art that I knew of—was a task of self-deception or decoration, a mere aesthetic flourish on the foundation of truth. I would see Maurizio Cattelan's *Comedian*, a banana duct-taped to a bare wall, and think, "These artsy fartsy people . . . Pffff." Or, I remember one interaction with an emerging musician. The musician was describing the excitement of his band, and I asked what kind of music they played. "Oh, it's hard to describe. We're not really accessible."

"Not really accessible?" I wondered. "Doesn't that mean you're just *bad*?"

I didn't "get" art until I came to the end of myself. I hadn't reached the end of theology, but I grew tired with theological articulation as I knew it. I was not as desperate as the philosopher John Stuart Mill, who was on the brink of suicide, but I could resonate with the futility of the logical life. John Stuart Mill's father attempted to train him as a master philosopher. He was educated by the world's best thinkers, started to learn classical Greek at age three, Latin at eight. He underwent the finest utilitarian education you could imagine. But in his early twenties, he became depressed. He knew he was intellectually mature but his emotions were underdeveloped. And you

22. John Paul II, "Letter to Artists."

know what shook Mill from his sadness? Beauty—specifically the poetry of William Wordsworth. Mill was a genius by most every measure, yet he was not fully formed. His soul needed fed, too, to beckon Mako Fujimura.[23] A purely logical life is limited.

Beauty opened Mill up to a deeper, more essential element of life. Pope John Paul II, again, is worth quoting:

> Every genuine artistic intuition goes beyond what the senses perceive and, reaching beneath reality's surface, strives to interpret its hidden mystery. The intuition itself springs from the depths of the human soul, where the desire to give meaning to one's own life is joined by the fleeting vision of beauty and of the mysterious unity of things. All artists experience the unbridgeable gap which lies between the work of their hands, however successful it may be, and the dazzling perfection of the beauty glimpsed in the ardour of the creative moment: what they manage to express in their painting, their sculpting, their creating is no more than a glimmer of the splendour which flared for a moment before the eyes of their spirit.[24]

This glimmer of splendor captivates both artist and the viewer. Beauty is compelling. Here is where the arts opened me up in a way that the world of modern theology couldn't. I couldn't explain or understand my way to God (try as I might). I realized I was more than a "thinking thing." The arts testified to the fullness of being human and to the range of human experience—and to the divine. I came to realize that the way I proceed with my reason is framed by beauty. The imagination is not childish but fundamental to being alive.

As Robert Jenson observes, "If we reflect upon something of beauty long enough, we should begin to be like it. If we study an image of horror or suffering, we will be moved to rage or pity. If these are only passing responses, we will not be truly changed. But if we are changed at all, if the images take root in us, we will act differently in the world."[25] Our beholding is our becoming, and artists can help people behold. They can help people like me see and pay attention to the nuance of life and the inexpressible. Sometimes, a theologian needs to be discipled by the artist.

23. Fujimura, "Culture Care."
24. John Paul II, "Letter to Artists."
25. Jenson, *Substance of Things Seen*, 21.

CONCLUSION: PARISH AND NIGGLE

J. R. R. Tolkien tells a tale of a painter named Niggle and his neighbor Parish. Tolkien was clear that he was not a big fan of allegory in interpreting his fiction, but I think that name "Parish," is purposeful.

Perhaps we could describe Niggle as the stereotypical artsy type: attuned to detail, "not very successful," because he had to spend his time with more practical matters. He was best at painting leaves, but his goal was to paint a whole tree. But the more he worked on the tree, the bigger it got. He became obsessed with making the perfect tree. But the more he wanted to work on and finish it, the more interruptions would come. This artist just can't get alone in the studio and do his thing without all these pesky worldly concerns.

Niggle didn't like his neighbor, Parish, very much, "partly because he was so often in trouble and in need of help; and because he did not care about painting."[26] Sound familiar?

There's another time crunch for Niggle in the story: he's preparing to leave for a journey. He knows this, so in the back of his mind, he's always racing against the clock to have enough time and space to work on his beloved painting that his neighbor can only see as "green and grey patches with black lines." Parish just doesn't get it.

Another issue with Niggle is that he has a kind heart: he feels obligated to help, and he feels compassion for those in need. You could say he's been morally formed by some story that incites him to see the needs of others. So as much as he wants to stay alone in the studio, he feels compelled to help when he can.

Some days Niggle has inspiration. It seems the days when he has inspiration, there are interruptions. An inspector comes and sees the sorry state of Parish's house, and then knocks on Niggle's door to see if he can help. He sees that he has canvas and wood and waterproof paint (which also happens to be his painting). But houses come first, not an impractical painting. At this moment of decision, a driver comes to take Niggle on his journey. He must leave his life unfinished.

When he gets to his destination (after passing through a stage of purgation), he's transported by train and then sees a bicycle at the gate with his name on it. He hops on and rides until at once he stops, awestruck. Here

---

26. Tolkien, "Leaf by Niggle," 101.

before him is "the Tree, his Tree, finished."[27] Opening his arms, he says, "It's a gift." There was the tree as he imagined it rather than what he made. And Niggle makes this observation: "Some of the most beautiful—the most characteristic, the most perfect examples of the Niggle-style were seen to have been produced in collaboration with Mr. Parish: there was no other way of putting it."[28]

After meandering in this forest for a while, looking around carefully and sensing enchantment, he comes to another realization about Parish. Parish was good at gardening, while Niggle's garden was a mess. To make this paradise park perfect, he needs Parish's help and advice on the things that Niggle does not know: tending earth, plants, and trees. They meet and begin to work. "As they worked together, it became plain that Niggle was now the better of the two at ordering his time and getting things done. Oddly enough, it was Niggle who became most absorbed in the building and gardening, while Parish often wandered about looking at trees, and especially at the Tree."[29] Eventually, Niggle looks farther to the mountains and desires to leave. Parish wants to stay and wait for his wife—to show her the countryside and see how she could improve it. At last, a man arrives to guide Niggle to the next destination. Parish asks the shepherd the name of this country.

"It is Niggle's Country. It is Niggle's picture, or most of it: a little of it is now Parish's Garden."

Shocked, Parish finally "gets" it. What they've been doing is cultivating the Tree and the Garden and the Place that Niggle imagined. Parish never realized the cleverness of Niggle; the picture never seemed as "real" as what he was now experiencing.

"He tried to tell you long ago" the man replied. "It was only a glimpse then . . . but you might have caught the glimpse if you had ever thought it was worthwhile to try."[30] At death, they see they needed each other, even if they never "got" each other in their earthly life. Niggle must restrain some of his creative freedoms because of his neighbor, Parish. Parish had to re-see what was worthwhile and necessary.

We need the Parish to help place us, to care for the earth as it is. And we need Niggle's to help us reimagine our place and what it could be.

27. Tolkien, "Leaf by Niggle," 107.
28. Tolkien, "Leaf by Niggle," 107.
29. Tolkien, "Leaf by Niggle," 108.
30. Tolkien, "Leaf by Niggle," 109.

The Joint/Joining Placemaking Work of Artist and Church—Jennifer Allen Craft

THE PRACTICE OF "PLACEMAKING" can be a transformative lens through which we understand ourselves as humans made in the image of a creative God, while also inviting deeper reflection on the communal relationship between the artist and church. This observation is grounded in four key claims. First, placemaking is a vocation and practice to which all humans are called in God's Creation. Second, the church, led by the Spirit of the divine Placemaker, is called to exercise this placed calling in a special way. Third, placemaking as a creative human activity can be witnessed paradigmatically in both the dispositions and practices of the artist. Finally, placemaking is therefore a generative way to understand the communal relationship and joint calling of the artist and church together for the world.

In the beginning, God makes places for all his creatures to dwell in harmony with one another—the sky, the seas, the land, and later the place of the garden of Eden, in which creatures share kinship and community in relationship with the land itself. Humans are, therefore, "emplaced" from the very beginning and invited to add our own creative marks to those places—naming animals, tilling and keeping the garden, and cultivating spaces to meet and experience God in particular ways. Being made in the image of God, we are called, according to Scripture, to reflect God's glory and divine placemaking work out into the world. Through our attentive, responsible care towards all of God's Creation, we model the work of the divine Placemaker, who actively and creatively engages with the world as an act of self-offering love.

As embodied creatures, we are shaped by place, and we actively shape place. We are active upon a place, but place is also a verb, as the Canadian artist Marlene Creates writes.[1] Place is active and powerful as God has

1. Creates, "Nature is a verb to me," 9.

gifted it to us. It forms a foundation for the way we see the world and in turn, how we will act within it. This reciprocal relationship is worth noting, as the theological question becomes not simply how we make places "better," but also how those places make us. If creation sings of God's glory, as the psalmist writes (Ps 19), then we would do well to listen and be formed by its music.

Our understanding of this placemaking work in God's creation is concentrated in the work of Jesus Christ, who makes a place among us, and later calls his church to join together places and people through the particularizing vision of the Holy Spirit. Christ comes to redeem "all things" (Col 1:15–20)—people *and* places—breaking cultural boundaries and inviting those at the edges of society and horizons of place to experience his presence in a unique way. The church, as image of Christ to the world, models this work of joining peoples and places into a new Spirit-led community identified with God's holy presence.[2] Within contemporary experience, this means that the church is called into the type of placemaking work that prioritizes the other, the outsider, the placeless, and the oppressed, decentering its own power and position in order to make room for everyone at the table of God. This will mean, practically, prioritizing placemaking work, as place forms the geographical location of boundaries, oppression, injustice, and ugliness. In order to join together in the reconciling work of the Spirit, in other words, the church must reevaluate its *actual* placemaking work in the world.

In order to do this, the church might look to the work of the artist, who models the work of placemaking in a unique way. In disposition as well as practice, the artist underscores the reciprocal and formative relationships we humans have to places more generally, while calling us into a particular performance of our holy placemaking work which the church desperately needs.

The placemaking work of the artist is revealed in both the *dispositions* common to the artist, as well as their creative physical *practices*. The artist regularly practices careful attention and curiosity for things of the world. In the process of seeing, of hearing, of touching, of speaking into reality the intricate details of the places around us, the artist works with attentive, loving presence. The outcome in the work of art often carries these ways of

2. Willie Jennings makes this point throughout his commentary on the book of Acts. The work of "joining" is a central image through which to understand the Spirit's work in community and our attendant calling as people who house the Spirit of God within us. See Jennings, *Acts*.

seeing the world and its communities within it, inviting viewers into the practice of careful attention and presence to an object, a contemplation of the love that animates one's appreciation for the world and its gifts. In this way, the work of the artist is, according to Rowan Williams, ultimately "the work of love."[3] This love is often grounded in the artists' love for the world around them and fosters, by way of result, affection, or love, in their audience.[4] This love has the potential, then, as it does for the artist themselves, to animate the church's placemaking practices and charge them with a holy curiosity to dig deeper into our places in responsible and reconciling ways.

The physical practices that result in the work of art also reveal the placemaking work of the artist. In their work, artists mix unexpected materials in ways that draw out beauty previously unrevealed. They carefully use their resources and materials, knowing their limitations, strengths, and weaknesses so as to make something that encapsulates what Nicholas Wolterstorff calls "fittingness" of both the object and practice.[5] As a model for the wider work of placemaking in the world, the artist teaches us the ways of conversation and responsible communion with the given, neither taking too much nor offering too little of ourselves to it. The work of placemaking is also never a singular endeavor. It is always a task formed in communion with past, present, and future members of a place. So it is also the case with artistic acts of making. Creative efforts are never purely the artist's own but are forged in communion and conversation with past and present voices, and oriented toward a future which, in Christian theological terms, sings of new creation.[6] In all these ways and more, the artist provides a particular picture of what placemaking work, both in disposition and practice, might look like in the world today.

Finally, then, I suggest that given our creative, shared identity as placemakers, we can begin to flesh out some important practical observations about the joint/joining work of the artist and church. First, the joint/joining work of the artist and church is supportive. At a time when artists often feel alienated from the work of the church in culture, the Christian church is called to "make a place" for the artist within community. The

3. Williams, *Grace and Necessity*, 164–65.

4. Wendell Berry argues that our placemaking work "all turns on affection." See Berry, *It All Turns on Affection*.

5. Wolterstorff, *Art in Action*, 96.

6. For more on this theme of the arts and new creation, see *Art of Creation*, edited by Begbie, Train, and Taylor.

church can, in this regard, support the placemaking work of the artist in a variety of ways, including developing their spiritual practice or providing patronage for their work in local communities. But this relationship, as was noted about the work of placemaking, is reciprocal. Artists should also find themselves supporting the placemaking mission and ministry of the church, offering up gifts and resources through which to better enable the creative endeavors of the church in its specific places.

The second relationship that emerges from this shared vision of placemaking is one of challenge. The church must allow the artist to challenge its own placemaking endeavors through the prophetic vision the arts offer. The church, as we know, is often complicit in the "sins of place" as much as it is in developing a redemptive "sense of place" in the world. The artist can challenge the ways the church sees it place and role in society by offering up new ways of seeing and hearing God's call to join together in the Spirit-led work of peacemaking and placemaking in the communities we inhabit. Churches can also challenge artists to expand their work beyond their normal areas of notice or involvement. In what ways can the church, then, challenge artists to join their work in ministries and missions that have been ignored? How can artists reimagine their work outside traditional venues for aesthetic contemplation and integrate their artistic practice into the church's wider work of placemaking in society?

Finally, a shared vision of placemaking creates a new identity that marks the relationship between the artist and the church—one of genuine partnership and joining in the work of God for the world. In this new identity, the church does not simply use artists for certain events or tasks. Neither does the artist simply see the church as one more potential venue for the expansion of their creative task. Instead, a real Spirit-led joining is made possible through the shared task of community placemaking. Both artist and church pursue the joint task of drawing congregations and communities into their places, and in so doing are joined together themselves in creative identity and embodied mission. The work of both church and artist, then, models the incarnational and Spirit-led work of Christ in and for the world. They dwell in the world richly and physically and imaginatively, participating in the redemptive placemaking work that God guides toward the New Creation.

May we then, as artists and creative members of God's church for the world, share in that hopeful vision of new creation as placemakers in the here and now, creatively offering ourselves in love to the world and listening for the Spirit's voice and calling in our particular places.

Conclusion

The artist has a special relationship to beauty. In a very true sense it can be said that beauty is the vocation bestowed on him by the Creator in the gift of "artistic talent." And, certainly, this too is a talent which ought to be made to bear fruit, in keeping with the sense of the Gospel parable of the talents (cf. Mt 25:14–30).

—Pope John Paul II

O God, whom saints and angels delight to worship in heaven: Be ever present with your servants on earth who seek through art and music to perfect the praises of your people. Grant them even now true glimpses of your beauty, and make them worthy at length to behold it unveiled for evermore; through Jesus Christ our Lord. Amen.

—Prayer for Church Musicians and Artists
(*Book of Common Prayer, 2019*)

Ok, one last Terrence Malick reference to close. As should be clear, we like Terrence Malick. We even like the movies that most of his fans don't like as much—like *To the Wonder*. In typical Malick fashion, *To the Wonder* features long, beautiful, sweeping clips of the countryside in the golden hour. The dialogue is sparse, other than some brief whispers of conversation. The film is a sort of montage between love beginning and dwindling and re-emerging and a priest doubting and struggling with faith. It's a difficult film without easy answers or explanations. Like most Malick films, it also takes time, which may be why many viewers are left unsatisfied.

In one storyline, Neil (played by Ben Affleck) falls in love with Marina (played by Olga Kurylenko) in Paris. Neil, a surveyor in the States, invites Marina and her ten-year-old daughter to come and live with him.

Their early, exciting love slows and steadies and is made more complicated by Neil's lack of commitment and Marina's expiring visa. Their passionate love leads to passionate conflict. Marina returns to France, and while she is there, Neil falls for an old high school friend, Jane (played by Rachel McAdams). The love affair fizzles out just as the one before, and Neil is left with another empty house. There's an air of loneliness experienced through loss.

We meet the other storyline through Father Quintana (Javier Bardem) when Marina and Neil return to the States after Paris. Marina seeks out marriage counseling, and we get a behind-the-scenes look at parish ministry as a celibate clergy member. We see the priest go out to the community and minister to the poor, illiterate, and diseased as he struggles with church conflict, failing marriages, and believing in God in the midst of pain, despair, and questions. There's an air of loneliness, though deep companionship, as he prays to the God he says he believes in. Both stories portray the passion of love, the gradual pain of loss, and the joy of redemption.

In many ways, *To the Wonder* is an allegory akin to the Song of Songs: two love stories at the same time. Many commentators often want to split the Song of Songs. Is it about the merely material relationship of marriage to be read like a manual? Or is it to be spiritualized to picture God's divine love and pursuit of humankind? With a sacramental imagination, we don't have to choose. It can be read on different levels, and both are true. It is a picture of marriage, and it is a picture of divine union, the material and spiritual, the manners and the mystery. We must not bypass either story; they enliven each other. The symbol of marriage reflects the divine relationship of love, doubt, and faithfulness.

In an early narrative of beauty, Plato features a dialogue between Socrates and Diotima about love—a theme fitting for Malick, the Song of Songs, and as we'll argue, making art with a sacramental vision. For Diotima, love starts with erotic desire.[1] We see someone physically beautiful, and we are attracted to them. But that's the mere physical or material level. If we consider beauty further, we appreciate physical beauty that is common in all the world rather than that one particular person. In other words, what are the common themes of beauty in the world? And if we go deeper still, we'd realize there is something better than physical beauty. We would experience a beautiful person without a beautiful soul. A beautiful soul is to be desired more than physical beauty. And if we take interior beauty further in, then we realize that there must be a Beauty in which all things

---

1. Plato, *Symposium*, 210c1–212a.

find their root. There must be a Form of the Beautiful in which beautiful things are made. The common beauty that all lesser beauties participate in is beyond sense or discursive reasoning. The arrival at seeing the surpassing worth of Beauty, or the beatific vision, starts with erotic desire, or love. It's an ecstatic and sudden encounter. There's an erotic shape to beauty and love. We become what we attend to.

This paradigm of beauty and love is the way God works. He woos us with his love, and we sort out our questions in the aftermath of the encounter. He doesn't answer all our questions as a great debater and convince us to believe. He compels us. Or in the concepts from Esther Lightcap Meek, we love in order to know.[2] We don't know in order to love. In the same way, as artists, we should be wooed and motivated by love and affection. We should love the good. This love of the good inspires our vision, for the pure in heart shall see God (Matt 5:8). We create out of love and for love. In a different context, Wendell Berry writes, "When work is done for love—of place where it is done, of the materials, the artistry, and the product of the work, of the people it is done with and for—then the sign or evidence of it will be beauty."[3] Beauty flows from love.

To bring back two familiar names, we want to end with Flannery O'Connor and Christina Rossetti and how their work is rooted in love. Commenting on the literature of O'Connor, Joshua Hren notices her attention. He writes, "Our realist contemplates these connections with intense interest, singing the contortions and conversions of our body and our souls not as an intermediary chorus like commentator, nor as an objective observer who has ascetically eliminated himself from the picture. He sees them with ardent affection, a lover of his readers and his characters who loves God still more, loves reader and character all the more for seeing both in light of their connection to the 'Love that moves the sun and other stars.'"[4] In a similar way, a sacramental artist has ardent affection, a love of his or her potential viewers and subjects.

Lastly, if anything is evident throughout Rossetti's writing, it is love—she describes in passionate terms both the joy and pain associated with loving deeply. She expresses her love for God in the poem "A Song for the Least of All Saints," saying, "Love is the key of life and death, Of hidden

2. See Meek, *Loving to Know* and *Doorway to Artistry*.

3. Berry, *Need to Be Whole*, 379.

4. Hren, *Contemplative Realism*, 58–59.

heavenly mystery: Of all Christ is, of all He saith, Love is the key."[5] Rossetti can often appear weary of doing good. Frequently, she expresses frustration with her ability to please God, and on occasion, she describes displeasure with what God calls her to do. She uses poetic terms to express emotions that all humans experience, but often repress to remain as unpublished thoughts. However, here she fulfills a poet's vocation, which is to provide words for the human experience, assuming that her grief is not unique to her own circumstances. In "Weary in Well-Doing," she writes, "I go, Lord, where Thou sendest me; Day after day I plod and moil: But, Christ my God, when will it be, That I may let alone my toil, And rest with Thee."[6]

Though she questions God in this poem, her knowledge of where rest is found never wavers. She describes the weariness associated with following God and the heartbreak that often comes with love. Moreover, she expands on the various elements of self-denial practiced in her spiritual life. These practices should not be considered as depriving her of a full life. Instead, they reveal the fullness of life that is found in giving up herself for the one she loves. She writes in "Weary in Well-Doing" that she continues to "go" where the Lord sends her, despite the struggles along the way, because she is convinced that rest is finally found in him.

Here, she reveals her life's purpose as loving God and finding fulfillment in his presence. Though she endured seasons of despair that led her to yearn for spring to arrive, Christina Rossetti found that even in sickness and heartache, at times, Christ provided the only reason for her to sing. While many consider her faith to have initiated much of her heartache, the difficulties she faced due to loss and illness may have done further damage had it not been for the hope that her faith provided. Rossetti writes in "The Thread of Life," "He bids me sing: O death, where is thy sting? And sing: O grave, where is thy victory?"[7]

Christina Rossetti's love for God is often misunderstood or falsely interpreted. Her work can be difficult to interpret unless the reader can identify with how the divine can capture one's heart. Georgina Battiscombe states, "Clearly the passion which she could find no satisfaction in her thwarted experience of eros spilled over into her expression of agape; but to explain her intense love of God simply in terms of repressed sex is too

5. Rossetti, *Complete Poems*, 454.
6. Rossetti, *Complete Poems*, 176.
7. Rossetti, *Complete Poems*, 331.

cheap and easy an answer."[8] Battiscombe remarks that for Christina, these two loves "were very closely akin."[9] In "Like As the Heart Desireth the Water Brooks," Rossetti writes, "My heart is yearning: Behold my yearning heart, And lean low to satisfy, It's lonely beseeching cry, For Thou its fullness art." She continues to describe her love for God in familiar terms that might otherwise be used to address a lover, "My heart is yearning, Yearning and thrilling thro', For Thy Love mine own of old, For Thy Love unknown, untold, Ever old, ever new."[10]

The attention given to the sensual nature of Rossetti's language points back to the struggle of modern interpreters to understand the depth of love that compels one to give up his or her life for another. Tennyson refers to the intense religious longing that characterizes much of Christina Rossetti's poetry. He states, "Put in the context of Tractarian poetics . . . her yearnings are the material from which poetry and art proceed."[11] In Tennyson's estimation, poetry is composed of the overflow of intense emotion, a characteristic that makes it effective.

BENEDICTION

We can't help but be priests. So, we'd like to send you off with a prayer and blessing. At the end of the liturgy each week, we say a closing prayer of Thanksgiving. We ask God to "send us out to do the work God has given us to do," which includes "to love and serve the Lord." That's our prayer for you as you close this book—that you be captivated by Jesus, that you attend to him, and that by attending to him, you may do the work that God has given you to do. For some of you that may be art-making. For others, it may be pastoring artists. For still others, it may be farming or homemaking or accounting. Whatever God has given you to do, we pray a sacramental imagination infuses your work as you participate with Christ in the world.

8. Battiscombe, *Divided Life*, 181–82.

9. Battiscombe, *Divided Life*, 112.

10. Rossetti, *Complete Poems*, 416–17.

11. Tennyson, *Victorian Devotional Poetry*, 203.

For Daily Growth   *Richard of Chichester*

Thanks be to thee, my Lord Jesus Christ, for all the pains and insults
thou hast borne for me, and all the benefits thou hast given me. O most
merciful Redeemer, Friend, and Brother: Grant that I may see thee more
clearly, love thee more dearly, and follow thee more nearly, day by day.
Amen.

Bibliography

Ambrose. "Isaac, or the Soul." In *Seven Exegetical Works*, translated by Michael P. McHugh. Fathers of the Church Patristic Series 65, 9–68. Washington, DC: The Catholic University of America Press, 1972.

Anselm of Canterbury. "A Meditation on Human Redemption." In *Anselm of Canterbury*, edited and translated by J. Hopkins and H. W. Richardson, 91–100. London: SCM, 1974.

Augustine. "Sermon 67 on the New Testament." Translated by R. G. MacMullen. In *Nicene and Post-Nicene Fathers* 6, edited by Philip Schaff. Buffalo, NY: Christian Literature Publishing Co., 1888. Revised and edited for *New Advent* by Kevin Knight. https://www.newadvent.org/fathers/160367.htm.

———. *The Confessions of St. Augustine*. Translated by E. B. Pusey. Oxford: James Parker and Co., and Rivingtons, 1876.

———. *The Trinity*. Edited by John E. Rotelle. Hyde Park, NY: New City, 2016.

Balthasar, Hans Urs Von. *Cosmic Liturgy: The Universe According to Maximus the Confessor*. San Francisco: Ignatius, 2013.

———. *The Glory of the Lord: A Theological Aesthetics, Vol. 1: Seeing the Form*. Edited by Joseph Fession and John Riches. Translated by Erasmo Leiva-Merikakis. San Francisco: Ignatius, 1982.

Barfield, Owen. *The Rediscovery of Meaning and Other Essays*. 2nd ed. San Rafael, CA: Barfield, 2006.

Battiscombe, Georgina. *Christina Rossetti: A Divided Life*. New York: Holt, Rinehart and Winston, 1981.

Baudrillard, Jean. *The Conspiracy of Art*. New York: Semiotext, 2005.

Bedford, Nancy Elizabeth. "The beauty of God: the senses, liturgy, and Christian discipleship." *Journal Of Latin American Theology* 7, no. 2 (2012) 37–59.

Begbie, Jeremy. *A Peculiar Orthodoxy: Reflections on Theology and the Arts*. Grand Rapids: Baker Academic, 2018.

Begbie, Jeremy, Daniel Train, and W. David O. Taylor. *The Art of New Creation: Trajectories in Theology and the Arts*. Downers Grove, IL: InterVarsity Academic, 2022.

Bell, Luke. *The Meaning of Blue: Recovering a Contemplative Spirit*. Kettering, OH: Angelico, 2014.

Bellah, Robert, et al. *Habits of the Heart: Individualism and Commitment in American Life*. Berkeley: University of California Press, 1985.

Bernthal, Craig. *Tolkien's Sacramental Vision: Discerning the Holy in Middle Earth*. Kettering, OH: Second Spring, 2014.

Berry, Wendell. "Christianity and the Survival of Creation." *Eco Faith Recovery*, January 4, 2011. https://www.ecofaithrecovery.org/wp-content/uploads/2012/09/BerryWendell_ChristianitySurvivalCreation.pdf .

———. *It All Turns on Affection*. New York: Counterpoint, 2012.

———. *The Mad Farmer Poems*. Berkeley: Counterpoint, 2008.

———. *The Need to Be Whole: Patriotism and the History of Prejudice*. Berkeley: Shoemaker, 2022.

———. *The Unsettling of America: Culture and Agriculture*. New York: Avon, 1977.

———. *Sex, Economy, Freedom and Community*. New York: Pantheon, 1992.

———. *A Timbered Choir: The Sabbath Poems 1979–1997*. New York: Counterpoint, 1999.

Boersma, Hans. *Heavenly Participation: The Weaving of a Sacramental Tapestry*. Grand Rapids: Eerdmans, 2011.

———. *Scripture as Real Presence: Sacramental Exegesis in the Early Church*. Grand Rapids: Baker Academic, 2017.

———. *Seeing God: The Beatific Vision in Christian Tradition*. Grand Rapids: Eerdmans, 2022.

Brenneman, Will. *Homespun Gospel: The Triumph of Sentimentality in Contemporary American Evangelicalism*. Oxford: Oxford University Press, 2013.

Brock, Sebastian. *The Luminous Eye: The Spiritual World Vision of Saint Ephrem the Syrian*. Collegeville, MN: Cistercian, 1992.

Brown, David, and Anne Loades, eds. "Introduction: The Divine Poet." In *Christ: The Sacramental World*. London: SPCK, 1996.

Brown, David, and David Fuller. *Signs of Grace: Sacraments and Poetry and Prose*. Fayetteville, NC: Morehouse, 1996.

Brueggemann, Walter. *The Land: Places as Gift, Promise, and Challenge in Biblical Faith*. 2nd ed. Minneapolis: Fortress, 1989.

Buechner, Frederick. *Wishful Thinking: A Seeker's ABC*. San Francisco: Harper, 2004.

Cameron, Julia. *The Artist's Way: A Spiritual Path to Higher Creativity*. New York: Tarcher, 1992.

Candler, Peter, Jr. "The Anagogical Vision of Flannery O'Connor." *Christianity & Literature* 60 (Fall 2010) 11–33.

Capon, Robert Farrar. *The Supper of the Lamb: A Culinary Reflection*. New York: Modern Library, 2002.

Clement of Alexandria. *Ancient Christian Commentary on Scripture, Mark*. Edited by Thomas Oden and Christopher Hall. Downers Grove, IL: InterVarsity, 1998.

Coleridge, Samuel Taylor. "The Statesman's Manual." In *Lay Sermons*, edited by R. J. White. Princeton: Princeton University Press, 1972.

Craft, Jennifer Allen. *Placemaking and the Arts: Cultivating the Christian Life*. Downers Grove, IL: InterVarsity, 2018.

Creates, Marlene. "Nature is a verb to me." In Susan Gibson Garvey, "Rephotographing the Land," 9–10. Halifax, Nova Scotia: Dalhousie Art Gallery, Dalhousie University, 1992.

Davies, Penelope, et al., eds. *Janson's History of Art: The Western Tradition*. 8th ed. London: Pearson, 2010.

Daniélou, Jean. *The Lord of History*. New York: Meridian, 1968.

De Lubac, Henri. *History and Spirit: The Understanding of Scripture According to Origen*. San Francisco: Ignatius, 2007.

———. *Medieval Exegesis: The Four Senses of Scripture.* Vol. 2. Translated by E. M. Macierowski. Grand Rapids: Eerdmans, 2000.

De Waal, Esther. *The Celtic Way of Prayer: The Recovery of the Religious Imagination.* New York: Doubleday, 1997.

Dickens, Charles. *Hard Times.* New York: Penguin Classics, 2013.

Dionysius. "The Divine Names." In *Pseudo-Dionysius: The Complete Works.* Translated by Paul Rorem. Mahwah, NJ: Paulist, 1987.

Edmundson, Mark. *Self and Soul: A Defense of Ideals.* Cambridge: Harvard University Press, 2015.

Fields, Stephen M. "The Beauty of the Ugly: Balthasar, the crucifixion, analogy and God." *International Journal Of Systematic Theology* 9, no. 2 (April 2007) 172–83.

Foltz, Bruce. *Medieval Philosophy: A Multicultural Reader.* New York: Bloomsbury, 2019.

Fraser, Hillary. *Beauty and Belief: Aesthetics and Religion in Victorian Literature.* Cambridge: Cambridge University Press, 1986.

Fuglie, Gordon. "Fade to Black: Decent Work by Duncan Simcoe." *Image Journal* 115. https://imagejournal.org/article/fade-to-black-recent-work-by-duncan-simcoe/.

Fujimura, Makato. *Art+Faith: A Theology of Making.* New Haven: Yale University Press, 2020.

———. *Culture Care: Reconnecting with Beauty for Our Common Life.* Downers Grove, IL: InterVarsity, 2017.

———. "Culture Care: Called to be Patrons." *Comment Magazine*, December 1, 2013. https://comment.org/culture-care-called-to-be-patrons/.

———. "Foreword." In *Doorway to Artistry,* by Esther Lightcap Meek, ix–xi. Eugene, OR: Cascade, 2023.

Gadamer, Hans-Georg. *The Relevance of the Beautiful.* Cambridge: Cambridge University Press, 1989.

García-Rivera, Alejandro. *Community of the Beautiful: A Theological Aesthetics.* Collegeville, MN: Liturgical, 1999.

Gilson, Etienne. *The Arts of the Beautiful.* New York: Simon and Schuster, 1965.

Gompertz, Will. *What Are You Looking At?* New York: Dutton, 2012.

Guite, Malcolm. *Faith, Hope and Poetry: Theology and the Poetic Imagination.* Oxfordshire, UK: Routledge, 2012.

———. *Lifting the Veil: Imagination and the Kingdom of God.* Baltimore: Square Halo, 2021.

Hauerwas, Stanley. *The Peaceable Kingdom: A Primer in Christian Ethics.* Notre Dame: University of Notre Dame Press, 1991.

Hauerwas, Stanley, and William Willimon. *Resident Aliens.* Nashville: Abingdon, 2014.

Hildebrand, Dietrich von. *Beauty in the Light of Redemption.* Stubenville, OH: Hildebrand, 2019.

Hopkins, Gerard Manley. *The Poems of Gerard Manley Hopkins.* N.p.: Digireads Publishing, 2018.

Horton, Michael. *Ordinary: Sustainable Faith in a Radical, Restless World.* Grand Rapids: Zondervan, 2014.

Howes, Graham. *The Art of the Sacred: An Introduction to the Aesthetics of Art and Belief.* New York: I. B. Tauris, 2007.

Hren, Joshua. *Contemplative Realism: A Theological-Aesthetical Manifesto.* San Francisco: Benedict XVI Institute, 2022.

Hume, David. *A Treatise of Human Nature.* New York: Dover, 2003.

Jennings, Willie James. *Acts*. Louisville: Westminster John Knox, 2017.

Jenson, Robert. *The Substance of Things Seen: Art, Faith, and the Christian Community*. Grand Rapids: Eerdmans, 2004.

John Paul II. "Letter to Artists." *Vatican*, 1999. https://www.vatican.va/content/john-paul-ii/en/letters/1999/documents/hf_jp-ii_let_23041999_artists.html.

Johnson, Junius. *Father of Lights: A Theology of Beauty*. Grand Rapids: Baker Academic, 2020.

Jones, David. *The Anathemata*. London: Faber and Faber, 1952.

Keble, John. *The Christian Year*. Oxford: Parker, 1949.

———. "Favor Shown to Implicit Faith." In *Sermons: Academical and Occasional*, 1–23. Oxford: John Henry Parker, 1848.

———. "Implicit Faith Recognized by Reason." In *Sermons: Academical and Occasional*, 24–42. Oxford: John Henry Parker, 1848.

———. *Lectures on Poetry*. Vol. 2. Oxford: Clarendon, 1912.

———. "On Reserve in Communicating Religious Knowledge." In *Tracts for the Times*, nos. 80 & 87, 1835–1836. London: Rivington, 1841.

———. "On the Mysticism Attributed to the Early Fathers of the Church" In *Tracts for the Times*, no. 89, 1835–1836. London: Rivington, 1841.

Kohlberg, Lawrence, and Rochelle Mayer. "Development as the Aim of Education." *Harvard Educational Review* 42 (1997) 449–96.

Kraut, Richard. "Aristotle's Ethics." In *The Stanford Encyclopedia of Philosophy*, Summer 2018 edition, edited by Edward N. Zalta. https://plato.stanford.edu/archives/sum2018/entries/aristotle-ethics/.

Küng, Hans. *Art and the Question of Meaning*. London: Crossroad, 1981.

Landow, George. *William Holman Hunt and Typological Symbolism*. New Haven: Yale University Press, 1979.

———. *Victorian Types, Victorian Shadows: Biblical Typology in Victorian Literature, Art and Thought*. Boston: Rutledge & Kegan Paul, 1980.

Lasch-Quinn, Elizabeth. "Ancient Philosophy's Return Amidst the Triumph of the Therapeutic." *Church Life Journal*, May 25, 2021. https://churchlifejournal.nd.edu/articles/ancient-philosophys-return-amidst-the-triumph-of-the-therapeutic/.

Lewis, C. S. "Bluspels and Flalansferes." In *Selected Literary Essays*, 251–65. New York: Cambridge University Press, 2013.

———. *The Great Divorce*. New York: HarperOne, 1973.

———. *Surprised by Joy*. New York: Harcourt, Brace & World, 1955.

———. *The Weight of Glory*. New York: Harper Collins, 1976.

Liddon, Henry. *Life of Pusey*. London: Longmans, Green and Co., 1893.

Louth, Andrew. "Beauty Will Save the World: The Formation of Byzantine Spirituality." *Theology Today* 61, no. 1 (April 2004) 67–77. https://doi.org/10.1177/004057360406100108.

Lundin, Roger. "Offspring of an Odd Union: Evangelical Attitudes toward the Arts." In *Evangelicalism and Modern America*. Grand Rapids: Eerdmans, 1984.

MacDonald, George. *The Complete Fairy Tales*. N.p.: Digireads, 2020.

———. *The Gifts of the Child Christ: Fairytales and Stories for the Childlike*. Grand Rapids: Eerdmans, 1973.

MacIntyre, Alasdair. *After Virtue: A Study in Moral Theory*. Notre Dame: University of Notre Dame Press, 1984.

Malick, Terrence, dir. *A Hidden Life*. Elizabeth Bay Production. Los Angeles: December 13, 2019.

——— *To the Wonder*. Brothers K Production. Los Angeles: April 12, 2013.

Maritain, Jacques. *Art and Scholasticism with other Essays*. Translated by Joseph Evans. New York: Scribner's Sons, 1962.

———. *Creative Intuition*. New York: Meridian, 1957.

McGrath, Alister. *Heresy: A History of Defending the Truth*. New York: HarperOne, 2009.

Meek, Esther Lightcap. *Doorway to Artistry: Attuning Your Philosophy to Enhance Your Creativity*. Eugene, OR: Cascade, 2023.

———. *Loving to Know: Covenant Epistemology*. Eugene, OR: Cascade, 2011.

Milliner, Matthew. *Mother of the Lamb: The Story of a Global Icon*. Philadelphia: Fortress, 2022.

Myers, Benjamin. *A Poetics of Orthodoxy*. Eugene, OR: Cascade, 2020.

Newbigin, Lesslie. *The Gospel in a Pluralist Society*. Grand Rapids: Eerdmans, 1997.

Newman, John Henry. *Apologia Pro Vita Sua*. New York: Appleton, 1865.

———. *Essays Critical and Historical*. Vol. 1. New York: Longmans, Green, and Co., 1907.

———. *An Essay in Aid of a Grammar of Assent*. London: Aeterna, 2014.

———. "On the Introduction of Rationalistic Principles into Religion." In *Tracts for the Times*, no. 73, 1835–1836. London: Irvington, 1839.

Nolan, James, Jr. *The Therapeutic Self: Justifying Government at Century's End*. New York: New York University Press, 1998.

O'Connor, Flannery. *The Habit of Being*. Edited by Sally Fitzgerald. New York: Farrar, Strauss, and Giroux, 1988.

———. *Mystery and Manners*. New York: Farrar, Strauss, and Giroux, 1979.

———. *A Prayer Journal*. New York: Farrar, Straus and Giroux, 2013.

O'Donohue, John. *The Invisible Embrace of Beauty*. New York: HarperCollins, 2004.

———. *Walking in Wonder: Eternal Wisdom for a Modern World*. New York: Convergent, 2018.

Packer, J. I. *Knowing God*. Downers Grove, IL: InterVarsity, 1993.

Pereiro, James, *'Ethos' and the Oxford Movement: At the Heart of Tractarianism*. Oxford: Oxford University Press, 2008.

Perl, Eric Justin David. "Symbol, Sacrament, and Hierarchy." *The Greek Orthodox Theological Review* 39, nos. 3–4 (1994) 311–56.

Pieper, Josef. *Leisure: The Basis of Culture (Including The Philosophical Act)*. Translated by Alexander Dru. San Francisco: Ignatius, 2009.

———. *Only the Lover Sings: Art and Contemplation*. San Francisco: Ignatius, 1990.

Plato. *Symposium*. Translated by Seth Benardete, with commentaries by Allan Bloom and Seth Benardete. Chicago: University of Chicago Press, 2013.

Prickett, Stephen. *Romanticism and Religion: The Tradition of Coleridge and Wordsworth in the Victorian Church*. Cambridge: Cambridge University Press, 1976.

Pusey, Edward. *An Historical Enquiry into the Probable Causes of the Rationalist Character Lately Predominant in the Theology of Germany*. London: Rivington, 1828.

———. *A Sermon Preached before the University of Oxford*. Oxford: Parker, 1867.

———. "Lectures on Types and Prophecies of the Old Testament." Pusey House Archive, Oxford.

———. *Parochial Sermons*. 2 vols. Oxford: Parker, 1852.

———. "Scriptural Views of Holy Baptism." In *Tracts for the Times*, vol. 2, 1834–1835. London: Rivington, 1840.

Reiff, Philip. *The Triumph of the Therapeutic: The Uses of Faith After Freud*. Chicago: University of Chicago Press, 1987.

Riches, John. "Balthasar's Sacramental Spirituality and Hopkins's Poetry of Nature: The Sacrifice Imprinted upon Nature." In *Christ: The Sacramental World*, edited by David Brown and Ann Loades, 1–15. London: SPCK, 1996.

Robinson, Marilynne. *Gilead*. New York: Picador, 2008.

———. *The Givenness of Things*. New York: Farrar, Straus, and Giroux, 2015.

Rorem, Paul. *Biblical and Liturgical Symbols Within The Pseudo-Dionysian Synthesis*. Toronto: Pontifical Institute of Medieval Studies, 1984.

Rossetti, Christina. *Rossetti: The Complete Poems*. Edited by R. W. Crump. London: Penguin, 2007.

Rubin, Rick. *The Creative Act: A Way of Being*. New York: Penguin, 2023.

Ruskin, John. *Modern Painters II*. Brookline, MA: Adament, 2000.

———. *The Mystery of Life and Its Arts*. New York: J. Wiley, 1869.

Russell, Norman. *Fellow Workers With God: Orthodox Thinking on Theosis*. Crestwood, NY: St. Vladimir's Seminary Press, 2009.

Sammon, Thomas. *God Who Is Beauty: Beauty as a Divine Name in Thomas Aquinas and Dionysius the Areopagite*. Cambridge: James Clarke & Co., 2014.

Sartre, Jean-Paul. *Existentialism Is a Humanism*. Translated by Carol Macomber. New Haven: Yale University Press.

Sayers, Dorothy. *Letters to a Diminished Church: Passionate Arguments for the Relevance of Christian Doctrine*. Nashville: Thomas Nelson, 2004.

Schellekens, Elizabeth. *The Aesthetic Value of Ideas*. Conceptual Art. Cologne: Taschen, 2005.

Seerveld, Calvin. *Rainbows for a Fallen World*. Toronto: Toronto Tuppence, 2005.

Shaw, David. "Poet of Mystery." In *The Achievement of Christina Rossetti*, edited by David A. Kent, 23–56. Ithaca, NY: Cornell University Press, 1987.

Sosler, Alex. "Ahhh I See: Educational Philosophy from 1 Corinthians 13:12." *Christian Education Journal* (October 2023). Forthcoming.

———. "Going to School with Marilynne Robinson: Sacramental Education as Alternative Paradigm to Faith Integration." *Christian Scholars Review* LII, no. I (November 2022). https://christianscholars.com/going-to-school-with-marilynne-robinson-sacramental-education-as-alternative-paradigm-for-faith/.

Sullivan, Lawrence. *Icanchu's Drum: An Orientation to Meaning in South American Religions*. New York: MacMillan, 1990.

Taylor, Charles. *The Malaise of Modernity*. Toronto: House of Anansi, 2003.

———. *A Secular Age*. Cambridge: Belknap, 2007.

Taylor, James. *Poetic Knowledge: The Recovery of Education*. Albany: The State University of New York Press, 1990.

Tennyson, G. B. *Victorian Devotional Poetry: The Tractarian Mode*. Cambridge: Harvard University Press, 1981.

Tolkien, J. R. R. "Leaf by Niggle." In *The Tolkien Reader*, 100–20. New York: Ballantine, 1978.

Vander Zee, Leonard. *Christ Baptism and the Lord's Supper: Recovering the Sacraments for Evangelical Worship*. Downers Grove, IL: InterVarsity, 2004.

Wallace, David Foster. "This Is Water." Commencement Address at Kenyon College. https://web.ics.purdue.edu/~drkelly/DFWKenyonAddress2005.pdf.

Weil, Simone. *The Need for Roots*. Translated by Arthur Willis. New York: Putnam, 1952.

Westerholm, Joel. "In Defense of Verses: The Aesthetic and Reputation of Christina Rossetti's Late Poetry." *Renascence* 51 (1999) 191–203.

Williams, Isaac. "On Reserve in Communicating Religious Knowledge." In *Tracts for the Times*, nos. 80 & 87, 1835–1836. London: Rivington, 1841.

Williams, Rowan. *Grace and Necessity: Reflections of Art and Love.* London: Morehouse, 2005.

———. *Looking East in the Winter: Contemporary Thought and the Eastern Christian Tradition.* London: Bloomsbury, 2021.

———. "Presence." *Art and Christianity* 43 (2005) 1–12.

Wolterstorff, Nicholas. *Art in Action: Toward A Christian Aesthetic.* Grand Rapids: Eerdmans, 1980.

Yannarss, Christos. *Person and Eros.* Translated by Normal Russell. Brookline, MA: Holy Cross Orthodox, 2007.

www.ingramcontent.com/pod-product-compliance
Lightning Source LLC
Chambersburg PA
CBHW032251070726
47590CB00016B/2372